Thomas Hutchinson, William Frederick Poole

The Witchcraft Delusion of 1692

Thomas Hutchinson, William Frederick Poole

The Witchcraft Delusion of 1692

ISBN/EAN: 9783337371982

Printed in Europe, USA, Canada, Australia, Japan

Cover: Foto ©ninafisch / pixelio.de

More available books at **www.hansebooks.com**

THE

WITCHCRAFT DELUSION OF 1692

BY GOV. THOMAS HUTCHINSON

FROM AN UNPUBLISHED MANUSCRIPT (AN EARLY DRAFT OF HIS HISTORY OF
MASSACHUSETTS) IN THE MASSACHUSETTS ARCHIVES

WITH NOTES BY
WILLIAM FREDERICK POOLE

———

BOSTON
PRIVATELY PRINTED
1870

THE WITCHCRAFT DELUSION OF 1692.

INTRODUCTION.

In May last I had occasion to consult the original manuscript of Gov. Hutchinson's second volume of the *History of Massachusetts*, which, it is well known, is among the Hutchinson papers in the State archives in Boston. I had never before seen the manuscript, and did not readily find the passage of which I was in search. The first portion of the manuscript seemed to be missing, and its place was supplied by matter which belonged to the Appendix. My first impression was that the missing sheets were those which Gov. Hutchinson did not recover after the stamp-act riot of 1765. Finding the matter of the Appendix out of place, suggested that the volume might have been carelessly arranged for binding. On collating the manuscript the early portion was found in another part of the volume. This was the copy used by the printers.

In my search I came to sheets which contained the subject matter of the printed text, but expressed in different language. I saw, on a closer examination, that this was an earlier draft, and the identical manuscript which had passed the ordeal of the riot of 1765 ; for portions of it were much defaced, and bore the marks of being trampled in the mud. The copy from which the volume was printed was evidently prepared at a later date. For the convenience of those who may hereafter consult this manuscript, I made in folio 7 (following the matter of the Appendix), the following memoranda :—

"There has been an error in binding this manuscript. The matter which precedes this is Appendix No. 1 (printed pp. 449–481, edition 1767, and pp. 404–423, edition 1795. The first portion of the history proper, ending with manuscript page 28 (to printed p. 40, edition 1767, and p. 43, edition 1795), has been placed in folios 92–100. Page 29 is opposite. This is the manuscript from which the second volume was printed.

"In folio 55 is the beginning of another manuscript, an earlier draft, from which the author prepared the narrative which appears in the printed vol-

1*

ume.   The earlier draft, ending in folio 91, carries the substance of the narrative to the word " Boston," on p. 313, edition of 1767, and p. 284, edition
of 1795.
    " These memoranda were made May 17, 1870 (with the approval of Mr.
Secretary Warner), at which time the earlier draft was first identified."
                                                                [SIGNED.]
    Both manuscripts are wholly in the autograph of Gov. Hutchinson, and
they seem to be prepared with equal care.   In form of expression and
phraseology they are quite unlike.   Incidents and opinions contained in the
earlier draft are changed, abridged and sometimes omitted in the later draft.
In matters of fact the earlier draft is often more precise and accurate than
the printed text, for the author doubtless prepared it with the original
authorities before him.
    The researches of Gov. Hutchinson into the early annals of Massachu-
setts are of the highest historical value.   He had opportunities of access to
original papers such as no person now possesses.   He had the tastes, the
capacity for close application and research, the judicial understanding and
the freedom from prejudice and partizanship which characterize the genuine
historian.   His style, if not always elegant, is clear and simple, and singu-
larly free from that sensational and rhetorical method of statement which is
the bane of much of the historical writing of the present day.
    Each of the several editions of Gov. Hutchinson's *History of Massachu-
setts* has become rare, and a new and revised edition will soon be demanded.
In the preparation of that work the earlier draft of the second volume,
which has now come to light, will furnish important materials.   For the
purpose of exhibiting the character and value of this manuscript, and for
contributing some additional information upon a special subject, I have ex-
tracted for publication that portion which treats the " Witchcraft Delusion
of 1692."
    So far as a presentation of facts is concerned, no account of that dread-
ful tragedy has appeared which is more accurate and truthful than Gov.
Hutchinson's narrative.   His theory on the subject—that it was wholly the
result of fraud and deception on the part of the " afflicted children "—will not
be generally accepted at the present day, and his reasoning on this point
will not be deemed conclusive.   That there were fraud and deception attending
it, no one will doubt ; but there is now a tendency to trace an analogy between the phenomena then exhibited, and modern spiritual manifestations.
No man of any reputation who lived in that generation, and saw what transpired at Salem Village and its vicinity, doubted that there was some influence then exerted which could not be explained by the known laws of
matter or of mind.   As these men left the stage, the theory of fraud was
gradually accepted by their descendants ; and at the period when Gov.
Hutchinson wrote, it was well nigh the universal belief among the educated
classes.

For the information of persons interested in tracing the resemblance between the abnormal manifestations of our time and those of the seventeenth century, I have appended notes to the other cases mentioned by Gov. Hutchinson, which may lead such inquirers to a further knowledge of their psychological phenomena.

The author's notes are indicated by stars, &c., and are signed H.   The editor's notes are indicated by numerals, and are signed P.   W. F. P.

———

On [mutilated][1] May, at a general council, there was an appointment of sheriffs, justices and other civil officers, and, among the rest, Commissioners of Oyer and Terminer for the trial of witches.   Upon this occasion the Governor suffered the council to choose the officers, and he gave or refused his consent to the choice—a mistake which no other governor has made, and which was giving up a right derived to him from the charter, the great difference between a nomination and assent being very obvious.

The old constitution being dissolved, it was absolutely necessary an Assembly should be called.   What was the rule of law in the meantime might be made a question; but at the first meeting of the General Assembly (the 8th of June) an act passed that all the laws of the Colony of Massachusetts Bay and the Colony of New-Plymouth, not being repugnant to the laws of England, nor inconsistent with the charter, should be in force to the 10th of November, 1692, in the respective colonies, except where other provisions should be made by acts of assembly; and all justices of the peace had the same power given them in the execution of laws which magistrates used to have.   No other acts were passed except two or three relative to the revenue; an act for erecting a naval office; another to enable the Governor, with the advice of the council, for six months to come, to raise and transport, or march the militia into either of the governments of Rhode Island, Connecticut, Narragansett or New-York; and another act for establishing a court of sessions of the peace, and inferior court of common pleas. The assembly was adjourned on the second of July to the second Wednesday in October.

The confusion occasioned by the supposed witchcraft seems to have been the reason why nothing more was done towards a body of laws better adapted to the new constitution; for on the 2d of June the commissioners held their special court at Salem.

---

[1] The council met on the 16th, 17th, 20th, 24th and 27th of May, 1692.   On the 27th the appointments named (of sixty-seven justices, eight sheriffs, and two coroners) were made. The twenty-eight councillors were also authorized to act as justices in their own localities. This injury to the manuscript was occasioned by its being thrown into the street during the stamp-act riot on the evening of August 26, 1765, when Gov. Hutchinson's house was sacked. In his subsequent draft, as the date was missing, he did not supply it, but said "At the first general council," &c.   This paragraph commences on page 8 of the manuscript.   P.

Before I relate their proceedings, I will collect, as far as I am able, the several instances of what was called Witchcraft, from the beginning of the country.

It is natural to suppose that the country, at the first entrance of the Europeans into it, afforded the most suitable scene, especially as a notion prevailed that the savages all worshipped the Devil; but I find no mention of witchcraft for the first twelve or fifteen years. About the year 1645,[2] several people in Springfield, upon Connecticut River, were suspected of witchcraft, and a greater number were supposed to be bewitched; among the rest two of the minister's children.[*] Great pains were taken to prove the facts upon the suspected persons; and about the year 1650, a poor wretch, Mary Oliver,[3] no doubt weary of her life, after long examination, was brought to confession. It does not appear that she was executed.

---

[2] The date named for the beginning of the Springfield troubles is probably three or four years too early. Gov. Hutchinson relied for the date of what he supposed to be the earliest witch case in the Massachusetts Colony, on Johnson's *Wonder Working Providence*, p. 199, where the date 1645 stands at the head of the page. As I have explained in my reprint of Johnson (pp. xiii.-xv.), these headings are unreliable, and, quite likely, were as often inserted by the printer as by the author. The date in the heading may be true as to some incident recorded on the page and erroneous as to other incidents. Keeping in mind the date when the work was written—from 1649 to 1651—the statement in the text involves no error. This portion was written in 1651. The author says, " There hath of late been more " than one or two in this town [Springfield] greatly suspected of witchcraft; yet have they " used much diligence, both in finding them out, and for the Lords assisting them against " their witchery, yet have they, as is supposed, bewitched not a few persons, among whom " two of the reverend Elders children." The cases came to examination and trial the same year the narrative was written, 1651, and the testimony offered covers the two previous years. P.

[*] Johnson. H.

[3] The name of this woman was not Mary Oliver, but Mary Parsons. She was tried in Boston, May 13, 1651, on the charge of witchcraft and for murdering her own child. She was convicted on the latter charge on her own confession, and sentenced to be hanged. She was reprieved till May 29 (Mass. Rec. iv. p. i. p. 47). In Judd's *History of Hadley* (p. 234), it appears that Mary Parsons was again tried for witchcraft in 1661, and discharged. This is doubtless an error in copying or printing 1661 for 1651, when the trial already named took place; for in both instances she was charged with bewitching the children of Mr. Moxon the minister. Mr. Moxon returned to England in 1652.

Hugh Parsons, her husband, had previously been tried and convicted of witchcraft; and the most damaging charges against him had been brought by his wife. Among these were the following:—1. Mrs. P. had an intimate friend Mrs. Smith, to whom she freely expressed her mind. Now Mrs. Smith was a person who went little abroad, and Mrs. P. was sure she would not speak of the secrets committed to her trust; and yet her husband knew all about their conversation. 2. He would be out late nights; and half an hour before he came home, she would hear strange noises about the house. 3. He would come home in a distempered mind, put out the fire, pull off the bed clothes, and throw peas about the house. 4. He would gabble in his sleep, have strange dreams, and say he had been fighting the Devil. The jury found him guilty. The magistrates set aside the verdict, and the case came before the General Court at Boston, May 31, 1652, when he was acquitted (*Ibid.* p. 96). The numerous and very curious depositions in the Springfield cases may be seen in the Appendix of Drake's *Annals of Witchcraft*, 1869, pp. 219-258. Hutchinson (in note, vol. i. p. 165) mentions the case of Hugh Parsons, but not that of his wife. He mentions it again (vol. ii. p. 22), and does not seem to be aware that his Mary Oliver case was that of Parsons's wife. My references to Hutchinson are to the edition of 1795. P.

Whilst this inquiry was making, Margaret Jones* was executed at Charlestown.⁴ Mention is made by Mr. Hale, of a woman at Dorchester,⁵

* Vol. i. p. 150. [Hutchinson's references to his earlier vol. are to the ed. of 1764.] H.

⁴ Margaret Jones was executed June 4, 1648, and was therefore by more than two years, so far as now appears, the first case of conviction and execution for witchcraft in the Massachusetts Colony. The case is reported in Winthrop's *Journal*, ii. p. 326, and Hale's *Modest Inquiry concerning Witchcraft*, p. 17. Mr. Hale relates incidents not recorded by Winthrop. On the day of her execution, he, then twelve years of age, went to her cell, "in company with some neighbors who took great pains to bring her to confession and re-"pentance; but she constantly professed herself innocent of that crime." P.

⁵ No writer on this subject seems hitherto to have given the name of the person who suffered at Dorchester. Mr. John Hale, in *Modest Inquiry*, 1697, p. 17, thus alludes to the matter: "Another that suffered on that account sometime after was a Dorchester woman. "And upon the day of her execution Mr. Thompson [Wm. Tompson], minister of Bran-"try and J. P. her former minister took pains with her to bring her to repentance. And "she utterly denyed her guilt of witchcraft, for she had when a single woman played the "harlot, and being with child, used means to destroy the fruit of her body to conceal her sin "and shame; and although she did not effect it, yet she was a murderer in the sight of "God for her endeavors, and shewed great penitency for that sin; but owned nothing of "the crime laid to her charge." Mr. Drake in his *Annals of Witchcraft*, and the *History of Dorchester*, make no mention of this case.

I think I have found a clue to the name of this Dorchester woman. Increase Mather, in his *Remarkable Providences*, 1684, gave some of the cases of witchcraft which had occurred in New-England. He sent a copy of this book to his brother Nathaniel, a minister in Dublin. In a letter, dated Dec. 31, 1684, Nathaniel Mather acknowledged the receipt of the book, and says: "Why did you not put in the story of Mrs. Hibbins witchcrafts and the dis-"covery thereof; and also of H. Lake's wife, of Dorchester, whom as I have heard the Devil "drew in by appearing to her in the likeness, and acting the part of a child of hers then "lately dead on whom her heart was much set; as also another of a girl in Connecticut, "who was judged to die a real convert, though she died for the same crime?—stories, as I "have heard them as remarkable for some circumstances as most I have read." (Mather Papers, *Mass. Hist. Coll.*, vol. xxxviii. p. 58.) Mr. Mather probably heard these stories before he went abroad. The precise date of his departure does not appear. It was, however, before March 23, 1650–51, when he writes from London. There was a Henry Lake residing in Dorchester in 1678, who, with his children, was named as the residuary legatees in the will of Thomas Lake, a prominent citizen of the town, who died Oct. 27, 1678 (*History of Dorchester*, p. 125). Mr. Savage (*Geneal. Dict.*) says there was a Henry Lake, currier, in Salem, in 1649, "who may have been the Henry Lake of Dorchester"; but he makes no mention of his wife being executed for witchcraft.

The details of the case as related by Mr. Mather are quite unlike those related by Mr. Hale. One or both of the statements must be incorrect. The error I think must be in that of Mr. Hale. Mr. Mather was a resident of Dorchester, and a graduate of the college in 1647. He gives the name of the person accused, and was so situated as to be familiar with all the incidents. Mr. Hale was a resident of Charlestown, and in 1650 was but fourteen years of age. He did not know the name of the person, and gives the same incidents to a Springfield case. He says, p. 19: "There was another executed of Boston anno 1656 [Mrs. "Hibbins] for that crime; and two or three of Springfield, one of which confessed, and said "the occasion of her familiarity with Satan was this: She had lost a child, and was exceed-"ingly discontented at it, and longed *Oh that she might see her child again!* And at last "the Devil in likeness of her child came to her bed-side and talked with her, and asked to "come into the bed to her that night and several nights after, and so entered into cove-"nant with Satan and became a witch. This was the only confessor in those times in this "government." If any person, other than Mary Parsons, was executed at Springfield for witchcraft, no details have come down to us. Increase Mather probably omitted to mention the cases of Mrs. Hibbins and Mrs. Lake, with which he must have been familiar, in deference to the feelings of their friends then living. P.

2

and another at Cambridge[6] about the same time, all denying what they were charged with. at their death ; and soon after Mrs. Hibbins*[7] the magistrate's widow, was executed at Boston.   In 1662, at Hartford, about 30 miles below Springfield. upon the same Connecticut River, one Ann Cole, whose father is said to have been a godly man who lived next door to a Dutch family, was supposed to be possessed by a Demon who sometimes spake Dutch and sometimes English, and sometimes an unintelligible language, the demons speaking in her things unknown to herself, and holding a conference, &c.   Several ministers who were present took the conference in writing with the names of the persons mentioned as actors ; and, among the rest, of a woman in prison upon suspicion. [one] Greensmith.   Upon examination she confessed also, and appeared to be astonished at the discovery, and owned that she and the rest had been familiar with a demon who had carnal knowledge of her. and though she had not made a formal covenant with him, yet she had promised always to be ready at his call, and was to have had a high frolick at Christmas, and then the agreement was to be signed.   The woman upon this confession was executed.†[8] Goffe, the Regicide, says in his diary, January 20, '62, that three witches were condemned at Hartford ; and afterwards, Feb. 24, that the maids were well after one of the witches was

---

[6] This was the case of Mrs. Kendal, of Cambridge, who was executed for bewitching to death a child of Goodman Genings, of Watertown.   The principal evidence was that of a Watertown nurse, who testified that the said Kendal did make much of the child, and then the child was well, but quickly changed in color and died a few hours after.   The court took this evidence without calling the parents of the child.   After the execution the parents denied that their child was bewitched, and stated that it died from imprudent exposure to cold by the nurse the night before.   The nurse soon after was put in prison for adultery, and there died, and so the matter was not further inquired into.   Hale's *Modest Inquiry*, p. 18.

Rev. Lucius R. Paige, of Cambridgeport, has recently found in the Middlesex court records, 1660, another alleged case of witchcraft in Cambridge, which was tried that year.   Winifred Holman, an aged widow, was accused by her neighbors. John Gibson and wife, their son John Gibson, Jr., and their daughter Rebecca, wife of Charles Stearns.   Actions of defamation were commenced against these parties, and on the trial, they, by way of justification, presented their supposed proofs of witchcraft, some details of which may be seen in *Hist. and Geneal. Register*, vol. xxiv. p. 59.   Probably other cases were tried in the courts of that period, of which nothing is now known.   John Dunton, in 1683, said there had been twenty cases of witchcraft recently tried in the colony. (*Letters*, p. 72.)   P.
* Vol. i. p. 187.   H.
[7] See *Mass. Rec.*, vol. iv. pt. 1, p. 269.   Joshua Scottow's representation, dated March 7, 1655-6, that he did not intend to oppose the proceedings of the court in the case of Ann Hibbins, is in *Mass. Archives*, vol. cxxxv. fol. 1.   She was executed June 19, 1656.   P.
† *Magnalia*.   H.
[8] The case of Ann Cole was fully reported in a letter by Mr. John Whiting, minister at Hartford, under whose observation it occurred, to Increase Mather, dated Dec. 10, 1682.   The document is one of the *Mather Papers*, and is printed in *Mass. Hist. Soc. Coll.*, vol. xxxviii. pp. 466-469.   An abstract of the case is in Increase Mather's *Remarkable Providences*, chap. v. pp. 96-99, London ed. 1856, and Cotton Mather's *Magnalia*, Hartford ed. 1855, vol. ii. p. 448.   Several of the incidents are not correctly stated by Hutchinson, either in the manuscript or printed text.   Ann Cole did not live next door to a Dutch family.   The name of the woman executed, Greensmith, appears in both abstracts by the Mathers, but not in Mr. Whiting's original statement.   The woman and her husband were both executed.   P.

hanged. In 1669, Susanna Martin, of Salisbury, was bound over to the Superior court upon suspicion of witchcraft, but discharged without trial.[9]

Another *ventriloqua*, Elizabeth Knap,[10] at Groton, in 1671, much as Ann Cole had done at Hartford, alarmed the people there. Her demon was not so cunning. He railed at the godly minister of the town, and at the same time uttered many blasphemous expressions; and then charged all her afflictions upon a good woman in the neighborhood. The woman had better fortune than perhaps as good an one had at Salem some years after.* The people would not believe the Devil, and Elizabeth confessed that she had been deluded, and that it was the Devil himself who tormented her in the shape of good persons. In 1673, Eunice Cole,[11] of Hampton, was tried, and the jury found her not legally guilty; but that there were strong grounds to suspect her of familiarity with the Devil.

In 1679, the house of William Morse,[12] of Newbury, was troubled with throwing bricks, stones and sticks, and playing so many pranks that he that believes the story told by Glanvil of the devils at Tedworth cannot avoid giving credit to this. It is worth observing that none of the family, except one boy, were afflicted. He was tossed about from one side of the room to

---

[9] This woman was one of the victims hanged for witchcraft at Salem, in 1692. The evidence offered at her examination is in Mather's *Wonders*, pp. 70–76; Calef's *More Wonders*, pp. 125–132, and Woodward's *Records of Salem Witchcraft*, vol. i. pp. 193–233. She bore the reputation of a witch for many years, and her suits at law frequently brought her name into the General Court records.—*Mass. Rec.* iv. pt. 2, pp. 540–555; v. pp. 6, 26.   P.

[10] To a person interested in the psychological inquiries pertaining to the witchcraft manifestations of the seventeenth century, the case of Elizabeth Knap is one of the most interesting that occurred in New-England. It took place twenty-one years before the great outbreak at Salem, and under circumstances which gave opportunity for calm observation. Samuel Willard, afterwards pastor of the Old South Church, in Boston, and who distinguished himself by his prudent conduct in 1692, was the pastor of the church in Groton at the time, and was the daily attendant and spiritual adviser of the family. He wrote a full account of the case, which fortunately has been preserved, and is now printed in the *Mather Papers*, pp. 555–571. In this paper he has calmly discussed the question whether her distemper was real or counterfeit. At first he was inclined to the latter opinion, and at times she confessed as much; but in view of all the facts he was of the opinion that there was something preternatural in the case. Increase Mather has an abstract of Mr. Willard's account in *Remarkable Providences*, p. 99. See also *Magnalia*, vol. ii. p. 449.   P.
* Rebeckah Nurse.   H.

[11] Complaints against Eunice Cole for being a witch were made as early as 1656, and were continued till 1680, when she was up before the Quarter Court at Hampton, and committed on suspicion of being a witch. During most of this period she was a town pauper. Thirty-five depositions and other original papers relating to Eunice Cole's case, from Sept. 4, 1656 to Jan. 7, 1673-4, are in *Mass. Archives*, vol. cxxxv. fol. 2-15. See also Drake's *Annals of Witchcraft*, pp. 99-103.   P.

[12] In the printed text Gov. Hutchinson gives but four lines to the Morse case. Fuller details may be found in *Remarkable Providences*, pp. 101-111; *Magnalia*, vol. ii. pp. 450-452, and Drake's *Annals*, pp. 144-150. In his Appendix (pp. 258-296), Mr. Drake has given depositions and other papers connected with the proceedings against Mrs. Morse. Other depositions, with a petition of Wm. Morse in behalf of his wife, are in *Mass. Archives*, vol. cxxxv. fol. 11-19.
Mrs. Morse was convicted 20 May, 1680, and sentenced to be hanged. June 1, she was reprieved till the next session of the court. "Nov. 3. The deputies, on perusal of the acts "of the honored court of assistants relating to the woman condemned for witchcraft, do

2*

the other, would have knives stuck in his back, and once one of them seemed
to come out of his mouth. He would bark like a dog, and cluck like a hen, and
once was carried away and could not be found for some time; but at length
was discovered creeping on one side, dumb and lame, and, when able to ex-
press himself said " that P——l[13] had carried him over the top of the house,
and hurt him against a cart wheel in the barn." Morse took the boy to
bed with him and his wife, and had the chamber pot with its contents thrown
upon them, and they were severely pinched and pulled out of bed, &c. These
things are related very seriously,* and it is a great wonder that P——l
escaped; for it does not appear that anybody suspected the knavery of the
boy.

In 1683, the demons removed to Connecticut River again, where the
house of one Desborough[14] was molested; and stones, earth, &c. thrown at
him, not only through the windows, but doors, by an invisible hand; and a
fire, kindled nobody knew how, burnt up no small part of his estate. It
seems one of Desborough's neighbors had a quarrel with him about a chest
of clothes which Desborough detained; and, as soon as they were restored,
the troubles ceased. All was charged upon the demons, and nobody, from
anything which now appears, suspected the honest neighbor.

In 1682, the house of George Walton,[15] a Quaker, at Portsmouth, in

" not understand the reason why execution of the sentence given against her by the court
" is not executed, and that her second reprieval seems to us to be beyond what the law will
" allow, and do therefore judge meet to declare ourselves against it, with reference to the
" concurrence of the honored magistrates hereto." This action was " not consented to by the
" magistrates." (MS. memoranda in Mass. Archives, vol. cxxxv. fol. 18.) The deputies
subsequently voted to give her a new trial; but the magistrates refused. Between this
disagreement of the deputies and magistrates she escaped punishment. She was released
from prison, but never acquitted or pardoned.   P.
    [13] Caleb Powel was the name of the person implicated.   P.
    * Magnalia.   H.
    [14] John Russell, minister of Hadley (in whose house the regicides Whalley and Goff
were long concealed), communicated this case to Increase Mather under date of August 2,
1683. It occurred the year before at Hartford. An abstract is in Remarkable Providences,
pp. 112-114, and Magnalia, vol. ii. p. 452. The original account is printed in Mather
Papers, pp. 86-88.   P.
    [15] An account of the Walton case was furnished to Increase Mather by Joshua Moody,
then minister at Portsmouth. (Mather Papers, p 361.) The paper is given in Remarkable
Providences, pp. 114-116, and Magnalia, vol. ii. p. 453.
    A long and circumstantial account of the disturbance in George Walton's house is the
subject-matter of a tract, printed in London, 1698, 15 pp. 4to., a copy of which is in the
Dowse Library belonging to the Massachusetts Historical Society. The title of the tract
is " LITHOBOLIA; or the STONE THROWING DEVIL. Being an exact and true Account of
" the various actions of Infernal Spirits, or (Devils Incarnate) Witches, or both; and the
" great Disturbance and Amazement they gave to George Walton's family, at a place
" called Great Island, in the Province of New-Hampshire in New-England. . . . By R. C.
" who was a sojourner in the same family the whole time, and an ocular witness of these
" Diabolic Inventions; the contents thereof being manifestly known to the inhabitants of
" that Province, and the persons of other provinces, and is upon record in his Majesty's
" Council Court held in that Province."
    The writer says, " Some time ago being in America, in his Majesty's service, I was lodged
" in the said George Walton's house, a planter there."
    The following names appear as attestants of the truth of the narrative: "Samuel Jennings,

New-Hampshire, was attacked in much the same manner. Walton had contention with a woman about a tract of land, and she was supposed to have done the mischief but by witchcraft.

About the same time another house was infested at Salmon falls[16] in New-Hampshire. And, in 1684, one Philip Smith,[17] a justice of the court,

"Governor of West-Jarsey; Walter Clark, Deputy-Governor of Road-Island; Arthur "Cook; Matt. Borden of Road-Island; Oliver Hooton of Barbadoes, Merchant; T. "Maul of Salem in N. E. merchant; Capt. Walter Barefoot; John Hussey and John "Hussey's wife." The narrative treats of throwing about, by an invisible power, stones, brick-bats, hammers, mauls, crow-bars, spits and other domestic utensils, for the period of three months.

"R. C.," the author of the tract, I have no doubt, was Richard Chamberlayne, Secretary of the Province of New-Hampshire in 1682. That he resided at Great Island appears by his signature to several depositions printed in *New-Hampshire Hist. Coll.*, vols. ii. and viii. Chamberlayne and Barefoot were among the prosecutors of Joshua Moody at Portsmouth the next year for not conducting his services according to the English Prayer Book, and occasioned his imprisonment for three months. It appears that Increase Mather was aware that Secretary Chamberlayne had prepared an account of the Walton case, and he wrote to Mr. Moody to procure it, together with a narrative of the Hortando case. Mr. Moody, July 14, 1683, writes to Mr. Mather: "About that at G. Walton's, because my interest runs "low with the Secretary, I have desired Mr. Woodbridge to endeavor the obtaining it; and "if he can get it, shall send it by the first; though if there should be any difficulty there-"about, you may do pretty well with what you have already." (*Mather Papers*, p. 359.) Mr. Moody writes again, August 23: "My endeavors also have not been a-wanting to obtain "the other [the Walton case], but find it difficult. If more may be gotten, you may expect "[it] when I come, or else must take up with what you had from me at first, which was "the sum of what was then worthy of notice, only many other particular actings of like "nature had been then and since. It began on a Lord's day, June 11, 1682, and so contin-"ued for a long time, only there was some respite now and then. The last thing [printed "*sight*] I have heard of was the carrying away of several axes in the night, notwithstand-"ing they were laid up, yea locked up very safe, as the owner thought at least, which was "done this spring. [Postscript.] Before sealing of my letter came accidentally to my hand "this enclosed that I had from William Morse of Newbury concerning the troubles at his "house in 1679. If it may be of use to me, you may please to peruse and return it." (*Ibid.* 360.)

The Secretary doubtless declined to furnish the unlovely Puritans at the Bay with his narrative, and, on returning to England, he printed it in London in 1698. The tract shows that Church-of-England men were quite as observant of signs and wonders as the Puritans. "Who that peruses these preternatural occurrences," asks the writer, "can possibly be so "much of an enemy to his own soul and irrefutable reason, as obstinately to oppose him-"self to, or confusedly fluctuate in, the opinion and doctrine of demons or spirits, and "witches?"

The tract is reprinted in *Historical Magazine* (N.Y., vol. v. pp. 321-327), and is followed (vol. vi. p. 159) with a statement, by Rev. Lucius Alden, on the persons and localities mentioned therein. Brewster's *Rambles about Portsmouth*, 2d series, 1869, has a chapter on the subject (pp. 343-351), with Mr. Alden's statement; but none of these writers seem to be aware that Richard Chamberlayne was the author of *Lithobolia*. Since writing the above I find the tract under the name of Richard Chamberlain in British Museum Catalogue, 1814, and the title was so copied into Watt and Lowndes.   P.

[16] This was the Hortando case, a brief narrative of which, "sent in by an intelligent person," is given in *Remarkable Providences*, pp. 116-118, and *Magnalia*, vol. ii. p. 453. "The enclosed I transcribed from Mr. Tho. Broughton, who read to me what he took "from the mouth of the woman and her husband, and judge it credible; though it be not "the half of what is to be gotten. I expect from him a fuller and further account before "I come down to the Commencement." (Mr. Moody to Mr. Mather, August 23, 1683. *Mather Papers*, p. 360.) The date, place and attending circumstances make it clear that this was "the narrative sent in by an intelligent person," which Mr. Mather printed.   P.

[17] Gov. Hutchinson found this case reported in *Magnalia*, vol. ii. p. 454.   P.

and representative of the town of Hadley, on Connecticut River, an hypo-
chondriac person, supposed himself to be under an evil-hand ; and suspected a woman, one of his neighbors ; and, continuing in that state until
he died, he was generally supposed to be bewitched to death.

In 1685, a large and circumstantial account of all or most of these instances was published,[18] and anybody who doubted the truth of them would
have been pronounced a Sadducee.

In 1688[19] begun a more alarming instance than any which preceded it.
Four of the children of John Goodwin, a grave man and good liver at
the north part of Boston, were generally believed to be bewitched. I have
often heard those who were then upon the stage speak of the great consternation it occasioned. The children were all remarkable for an ingenui-
ty of temper, had been religiously educated, and were supposed to be
incapable of imposture or fraud. The eldest was a girl about thirteen years
of age, it is said, it may be something more. She had charged a laundress
with taking away some of the family linen. The mother of the laundress
was one of the wild Irish, and gave the girl very bad language ; after which
she fell into a sort of fits, which were said to have something diabolical in
them. One of her sisters and two of her brothers, whose ages were not
transmitted,[20] soon followed her example, and they are said to have been
tormented in the same parts of their bodies at the same time, though kept
at a distance so as not to know one another's complaints. One thing was
remarkable, and ought to have been taken more notice of, that all
their complaints were in the day time, and that they slept comfortably all
night. They were sometimes deaf, then dumb, then blind, and sometimes
all these together. Their tongues would be drawn down their throats, then
pulled out upon their chins. Their jaws, necks, shoulders, elbows, and all
their joints would appear to be dislocated, and they would make the most
piteous outcries of being cut with knives and beat ; and plain marks of
wounds might afterwards be discovered. The ministers of Boston and
Charlestown kept a day of fasting and prayer at the troubled house ; and
after that the youngest child made no more complaints. But the magistrates

[18] Increase Mather's *Remarkable Providences* is the work here alluded to ; but the date
should have been 1684 and not 1685. The book was issued in the Spring of 1684.
Nathaniel Mather, in a letter to the author, dated Dec. 31, 1684, acknowledges receiving a
copy on which "was written in your hand 7 ber 16." (*Mather Papers*, p. 58.) John Bishop
acknowledges the receipt of a copy, in a letter dated June 10, 1684. (*Ibid.* p. 312.) This
erroneous date, and a typographical error in the *Magnalia*, vol. ii. p. 473, have led some
writers to suppose that Cotton Mather wrote his first book on witchcraft in 1685. He was
then twenty-two years of age. Before 1686 he published no works except *Elegy on Rev.
Nath. Collins*, 1685, and *The Boston Ephemeris*, an Almanac for 1683, neither of which are
in the printed list of his works. His first writing on witchcraft was issued in 1689.   P.
[19] This date is correct. It is singular that in his final draft the author should be in doubt,
and say, "in 1687 or 1688."   P.
[20] The names and ages of the children were as follows : Martha 13, John 11, Mercy 7,
Benjamin 5.   P.

unfortunately interposed; and the old woman was apprehended, examined, committed and brought to trial, and seems neither to have owned nor denied her guilt, being either really a distracted person, or endeavoring to appear such; and, before sentence of death was passed, the opinion of physicians was taken; but they returned that she was *compos mentis*, and she was executed, declaring at her death the children should not, or perhaps it might be, would not be relieved by her death, and that others besides her had a hand in their afflictions. This no doubt came to the children's knowledge; and their complaints immediately increased beyond what they had ever been before. As this relation is in print,[21] and but few persons have doubted that there was a preternatural agency in the case of these children, and [as] Mr. Baxter, in a preface to an edition published in London, says: " the evidence is so convincing that he must be a very obdurate Sadducee who will not believe," I will spend a little more time in examining it, than otherwise I should think convenient.

The eldest is after this the principal subject; and was taken into a minister's[22] family, where for some days she behaved orderly, but after that suddenly fell into her fits. The relation chiefly consists of their being violently beaten by specters; put into red hot ovens, and their sweating and panting; having cold water thrown upon them, and then shivering; being roasted

---

[21] Cotton Mather's *Memorable Providences*, Boston, 1689. 2d ed. London, 1691.   P.
[22] Cotton Mather's. On the 4th of October, 1688, Joshua Moody wrote a letter to Increase Mather, then in London, in which he spoke of the Goodwin case. (*Mather Papers*, pp. 367-8.) He says " We have a very strange thing among us, which we know not what " to make of, except it be witchcraft, as we think it must needs be. Three or four children " of one Goodwin, a mason, that have been for some weeks grievously tormented, crying " out of head, eyes, tongue, teeth; breaking their neck, back, thighs, knees, legs, feet, " toes, &c.; and then they roar out, *Oh my head! Oh my neck!* and from one part to an- " other the pain runs almost as fast as I write it. The pain is doubtless very exquisite, and " the cries most dolorous and affecting; and this is notcable, that two or more of them cry " out of the same pain in the same part, at the same time, and as the pain shifts to another " place in one, so in the other, and thus it holds them for an hour together and more; and when " the pain is over they eat, drink, walk, play, laugh, as at other times. They are generally well " a nights. A great many good Christians spent a day of prayer there. Mr. Morton came " over, and we each spent an hour in prayer; since which, the parents suspecting an old woman " and her daughter living hard by, complaint was made to the justices, and compassion had " so far, that the women were committed to prison and are there now. Yesterday I called " in at the house, and was informed by the parent that since the women were confined the " children have been well while out of the house; but as soon as any of them come into " the house, then taken as formerly; so that now all their children keep at their neigh- " bors' houses. If any step home they are immediately afflicted, and while they keep out " are well. I have been a little larger in this narrative because I know you have " studied these things. We cannot but think the Devil has a hand in it by some instru- " ment. It is an example, in all the parts of it, not to be paralelled. You may inquire " farther of Mr. Oakes [Edward, Jr., the bearer of the letter], whose uncle [Dr. Thomas " Oakes] administered physic to them at first, and he will probably inform you more fully."
We have here a motive other than curiosity or credulity, which led Mr. Mather to take one of the Goodwin children to his own house, where he kept her till spring and till she fully recovered. This letter of Mr. Moody's was prior to any writing on the subject by Mr. Mather. An account of this case is in the *Magnalia*, vol. ii. pp. 456-465. See also *North American Review*, vol. cviii. pp. 350-359.   P.

upon invisible spits ; having their heads nailed to the floor, so as that they could hardly be pulled away ; their joints first stiff and then limber ; pins stuck into their flesh; choaked until they were black in the face ; having the witches invisible chain upon them; dancing with a chair, like one riding on horseback; being able to read bad books, and blind if they looked into a good one ; being drunk without anything to intoxicate.

There is nothing in all this but what may be accounted for from craft and fraud, which children of that age are very capable of; or from agility of body, in which these children are exceeded by common tumblers much younger. There are some instances mentioned of another sort, namely : of their being tormented when any person took up a bible to look into it whilst the children were in the room, although their faces were another way, and they could not see it until it was laid aside; their telling of plate at the bottom of the well, which, it is said, they had never heard of before— and yet, in fact, plate had been lost there; of their eyes being put out when they were told to look to God, not only in English, but in Latin, Greek, or Hebrew; whereas from the Indian language no such effect followed, the Devil being said not to have understood that language[23]—all which serve only to evidence the inattention and the strong prejudice in favor of the children in those who were their observers. The strangest circumstance of all is that the children, after their return to their ordinary behavior, made profession of religion, and reckoned their affliction among the incentives to it. One of them was, many years after, one of my tenants, a grave, religious woman, [and] was never known to have made any confession of fraud, probably was never charged with it. But even all this is not miraculous.*[24] The account of this affair being made public obtained general credit.

[23] A friend skilled in the Indian dialects suggests that Mr. Mather's pronunciation of the Indian language was probably so imperfect that the Devil was excusable for not understanding it.   r.

* In the year 1720, at Littleton, in the Massachusetts Province, a family were supposed to be bewitched in much the same manner with this of Goodwin's. I shall give a brief account of the affair, and the manner how the fraud came to be disclosed, to show the similitude between the two cases, and to discourage parents from showing the least countenance to such pranks in their children.

One J. B. of Littleton, had three daughters of 11, 9, [and] 5 years of age. The eldest being a forward girl, and having heard and read many strange stories, used to surprise the company where she was with her manner of relating them. Pleased with applause she went from stories to dreams, and from dreams to visions, attaining the art of swooning away, and being to all appearance breathless for some time; and upon her reviving would tell strange stories of what she had met with in this and other worlds. When she met with the words God, Christ or Holy Ghost in the Bible, she would drop down with scarce any signs of life in her. Strange noises were heard in the house, stones came down the chimney and did great mischief. It was common to find her in ponds of water, crying out she should be drowned, sometimes upon the top of the house, and sometimes upon the tops of trees, and, being asked, said she flew there; complained of beating and pinching by invisible hands which left the marks upon her. She complained of a woman of the town, one Mrs. D—y, and that she appeared to her, and once her mother struck at the place where

44444444444

the country for his gravity and piety, and his favorable opinion of the old Puritanism, as much as for his knowledge in the law. The trials of the witches in Suffolk had been published not long before.[31] The evidence here was of the same sort with what had been judged sufficient to hang people there. Reproach then for hanging witches, although it has been often cast upon the people of New-England by those of Old-, yet it must have been done with an ill grace. We had their best authority to justify us; besides the prejudices of education [and] disposition from thence to give a serious, solemn construction to even common events in Providence, might be urged as an excuse here in some measure; but in England this was an age of as great gaiety as any age whatever, and of as great infidelity in general as any which preceded it.

Sir William Phips, the Governor just arrived,[32] seems to have given in to the prevailing opinion. He was much under the direction of the spiritual fathers of the country. Mr. Stoughton, the Lieut. Governor, and at the head of the Court[33] for trial of the witches, and who had great influence upon the rest of the judges, had taken up this notion that, although the Devil might appear in the shape of a guilty person, yet he would never be permitted to assume the shape of an innocent person.[*] This opinion, at first, was generally received and would not bear to be contradicted. Some of the most religious women who were accused, when they saw the appearance of distress and torture in the girls, and heard their solemn declarations that they saw the shapes or specters of the accused afflicting them, persuad-

witchcraft in New-England. An abstract of the case is in *Wonders of the Invisible World*, pp. 55–60; and allusions to the same are found in nearly all subsequent treatises on witchcraft. It is perhaps the most noted case on record, as Sir Matthew Hale here sanctioned by his great name the admission of spectral evidence, and the dogma that the devil could act only through persons in league with him, that is, actual witches. In the Dowse Library is "A Discourse concerning the great mercy of God in preserving us from the Power and "Malice of Evil Angels; written by Sir Matthew Hale, at Cambridge 26 March 1661 [1665], "upon occasion of a Tryal of certain Witches before him the week before at St. Edmund's "Bury." London, 1693. 4to.   P.
[31] 1684.   P.
[32] Sir William Phips arrived at Boston, May 14, 1692. Increase Mather returned from his four years' mission as colonial agent in England, in the same vessel.   P.
[33] The organization and commission of the court is given in note 44.   P.
[*] "A gentleman of more than ordinary understanding, learning and experience, desired "me to write to New-England about your trials and convictions of witches; not being "satisfied with the evidence upon which some who have been executed were found "guilty. He told me, that in the time of the great reformation parliament, a certain per- "son or persons had a commission to discover and prosecute witches. Upon these prose- "cutions many were executed, in at least one county in England, until, at length, a gentle- "man of estate and of great character for piety was accused, which put an end to the com- "mission. And the judges upon a re-hearing, reversed many judgments; but many lives "had been taken away. All that I speak with much wonder that any man, much less a "man of such abilities, learning and experience as Mr. Stoughton, should take up a per- "suasion, that the devil cannot assume the likeness of an innocent, to afflict another person. "In my opinion, it is a persuasion utterly destitute of any solid reason to render it so much "as probable, and besides, contradictory to many instances of fact in history. If you think "good, you may acquaint Mr. Stoughton and the other judges with what I write." *Letter from London to I. Mather*, Jan. 9, 1692-3.   H.

ed themselves they were witches, and that the Devil, somehow or other, though they could not remember when, had taken possession of their evil hearts, and obtained some sort of assent to his afflicting in their shapes; and thereupon they confessed themselves to be guilty.

Even to this day, the country seems rather to be divided in opinion whether it was the accused or the afflicted who were under some preternatural or diabolical possession, than whether the afflicted were under bodily distempers, or altogether guilty of fraud and imposture.

The trial of Richard Hatheway,[34] before Lord Chief Justice Holt, opened the eyes of all except the lowest part of the people in England; and an act of Parliament in his late Majesty's reign[35] will prevent the prejudice which remains in them from the mischiefs it used to produce on juries in judicial proceedings. It is a great pity the like examples of conviction and punishment had not been made here. I hope an impartial narrative of the supposed witchcrafts at Salem will convince the New-England reader that there was no thing preternatural in the whole affair; but all proceeded from the most amazing wickedness of the accusers.

In February, 1691 [-2], a daughter and a niece of Mr. Parris,[36] the minister

[34] Richard Hatheway, a blacksmith's apprentice, was tried before chief justice Holt, March 25, 1702, for imposture. He pretended to be bewitched by Sarah Morduck, and to be restored from his fits only by drawing blood from her by scratching. She had been tried for witchcraft by the same court the year before, and acquitted. He pretended to vomit pins, and to fast for ten weeks. "All the devils in hell," said the chief justice, "could not have helped you fast so long." Pins were found in his pocket; and being closely watched, it was ascertained that he partook of food when he assumed to be fasting. Another woman was brought in while he was in his fits, and by scratching her he recovered as well as before. He was sentenced to imprisonment for one year, and to stand in the pillory three times. Rev. Francis Hutchinson states the case in *Historical Essay concerning Witchcraft*, London 2d edition, 1720, p. 280, and it appears in *Wonders of the Invisible World*, pp. 55 and 60. The case with the evidence and arguments is reported in Howell's *State Trials*, vol. xiv. pp. 639-669. Hatheway's master and mistress, who sustained the apprentice in these impostures, were next prosecuted for assault on Sarah Morduck and for riot; and their trial is reported in the same volume.

Howell's *State Trials* contain full reports of other witchcraft proceedings, viz.: Case of Mary Smith, 1616, vol. ii. p. 1050; Proceeding against the Essex Witches, 1645, vol. iv. p. 817; and Proceedings against three Devon Witches, 1682, vol. viii. p. 1018.   P.

[35] Eleven trials for witchcraft were held before chief justice Holt, from 1694 to 1702, in which he so charged the juries that they generally brought in verdicts of acquittal. The English statutes for the punishment of witchcraft, however, were not repealed till 1736. 9 Geo. II. chap. 5, *Statutes at Large*, vol. xvii. p. 3.   P.

[36] "An Account of the Life and Character of Rev. Samuel Parris, of Salem village, and " of his connection with the Witchcraft Delusion of 1692. By Samuel P. Fowler [of Dan- " vers]" (Salem, 1857, 20 pp. 8vo.), is the fullest and most impartial estimate of Mr. Parris's character which has appeared in print. Deacon Fowler is an officer of the original church of Salem village, now Danvers; he has the best collection of witch books in New-England, and is one of the most experienced antiquaries of the Essex Institute. He dispels much of the misapprehension which has existed respecting this noted clergyman.

Mr. Parris remained with his people for five years after these events, and in the midst of local disputes outside of the witchcraft tragedy. Mr. Fowler says (p. 19), "It seems there " was always a majority of the parish in favor of Mr. Parris remaining with them; and " there appears to have been a very general mistake with regard to his dismission from his " people, they supposing that he was hastily driven away from the village; whereas he

of Salem village, girls of ten or eleven years of age, and one or two more
girls in the neighborhood, made the same sort of complaints as Goodwin's
children had done two or three [four] years before.   The physicians, having
no other way of accounting for the disorder, pronounced them bewitched. An
Indian woman who lived with the minister, with her husband,[37] tried an ex-
periment to find out the witch.   This coming to the children's knowledge,
they cried out upon the Indian woman as appearing to them, pinching,
pricking and tormenting them, and fell into fits, became convulsed, dis-
torted, &c.

Tituba, the name of the woman, who was a Spanish Indian, as some
accounts tell us, owned that her mistress had taught her in her own country how to find out a witch ; but she denied her being one herself.   Several
private fasts were kept at the minister's house, and several more by the
whole village, and by neighboring parishes, and a public fast through
the colony to seek to God to rebuke Satan, &c.   Soon after the number
of the complainants increased, and among them girls, two or three women, and some old enough to be admitted witnesses.   These had their fits
too, and cried out, not only upon Tituba, but upon an old melancholy distracted woman, Sarah Osburn, and a bed-rid old woman, Sarah Good.
Tituba, urged to it by her master as she afterwards declared,* confessed
herself a witch, and that the two old women were confederates with her, and
thereupon they were all committed to prison ; and Tituba being searched
was said to have the marks of the Devil's wounding her upon her body,†
but more probably of Spanish cruelty.   This was the first of March. About
three weeks after two other women who were church-members and of good
character, [Martha] Corey and [Rebecca] Nurse, were complained of, examined and would confess nothing, but were committed.   Not only the
three children, while the women were under examination, fell into their fits
and had all their complaints, but the mother of one of the children and wife
of Thomas Putnam complained of Nurse as tormenting her, and made most
terrible shrieking to the amazement of all in the neighborhood.   Such was

" continued and maintained himself through a ministerial quarrel of five years, until he
" saw fit to discontinue it, when he informed his church of his intentions."

Mr. Fowler's entire paper is reprinted in Mr. Drake's *Witchcraft Delusion in New-England*, vol. iii. pp. 198-221.   The anonymous Ballad of 1692, *Giles Corey and Goodwyfe
Corey*, which Mr. Drake reprints in the same volume (pp. 173-177), and supposes Mr. J. G.
Whittier to have been the author—" as but one person could have written it "—was contri-
buted to a Salem newspaper, more than thirty years ago, by Mr. Fitch Poole, of Danvers,
now librarian of the Peabody Institute in Peabody.   P.

[37] John Indian and his wife Tituba were slaves.   In the mittimus to the jail keeper at
Boston, she is described as " an Indian woman belonging to Samuel Parris of Salem village."
(Woodward's *Records of Salem Witchcraft*, vol. i. p. 15.)   Calef (p. 19) says, " she lay in
" jail till sold for her fees."   The Salem delusion had its origin in the fetichism practised
by these two ignorant Spanish-African slaves, whom Mr. Parris probably obtained from the
Barbadoes, where he was at one time in business.   P.

* R. Calef. [*More Wonders*, p. 91.]   H.
† Hale. [*Modest Inquiry*, p. 25, ed. 1711.]   H.

the infatuation that a child* of Sarah Good, not above four or five years old, was committed also, being charged with biting the afflicted who showed the print of small teeth upon their arms.

Soon after, April 3, Sarah Cloyse, sister to Nurse, being at meeting, and Mr. Parris taking for his text John vi. 70, "Have not I chosen you twelve, and one of you is a Devil?" she was offended and went out of meeting, and she was soon after complained of, examined and committed; and about the same time Elizabeth Proctor was charged; and, her husband accompanying her to her examination, he was complained of also, and both committed. The great imprudence, to say the best of it, in those who were in authority [Hathorne and Corwin, local magistrates], in encouraging and putting words into the mouths of the accusers, or suffering others to do it, will appear by the examination of these persons remaining upon the files of the court. The accusers and accused were brought before the court. Mr. Parris, who had been over-officious from the beginning, was employed to examine these,[38] and most of the rest of the accused.

At a court[39] held at Salem, 11th April, 1692, by the honoured Thomas Danforth, deputy governor. Q. John (i. e. the Indian), who hurt you? A. Goody Proctor first, and then Goody Cloyse. Q. What did she do to you? A. She brought the book to me. Q. John, tell the truth, who hurts you? Have you been hurt? A. The first was a gentlewoman I saw. Q. Who next? A. Goody Cloyse. Q. But who hurt you next? A. Goody Proctor. Q. What did she do to you? A. She choked me, and brought the book. Q. How oft did she come to torment you? A. A good many times, she and Goody Cloyse. Q. Do they come to you in the night as well as the day? A. They come most in the day. Q. Who? A. Goody Cloyse and Goody Proctor. Q. Where did she take hold of you? A. Upon my throat, to stop my breath. Q. Do you know Goody Cloyse and

* Calef. [p. 92.]   R.

[38] This statement is a mistake, and is changed in the final draft. Mr. Parris on no occasion was employed to examine the accused. At the request of the magistrates he took down the evidence, he being a rapid penman and stenographer. On the occasion mentioned in the next paragraph, Danforth put the questions, and the record is, "Mr. Parris being de-"sired and appointed to write out the examination, did take the same, and also read it be-"fore the council in public."   P.

[39] This was a meeting of the council for a preliminary examination, and not "a court" for the trial of the accused. Danforth, deputy governor; Addington, secretary, and Russell, Hathorne, Appleton, Sewall and Corwin, members of the council, were present. It was the only examination that Samuel Sewall attended. On his return to Boston he made this entry in his diary: "April 11, 1692. Went to Salem, where, in the meeting house, the "persons accused of witchcraft were examined; was a very great assembly; 'twas awful "to see how the afflicted were agitated." At a later date he inserted in the margin, " Væ, "væ, væ." These words have been taken by a late writer "as expressions of much sensibility "at the extent to which he had been misled." He did in later years regret, and well he might, the course he took in the witchcraft trials; but he never expressed, as the writer does, his disbelief in the reality of diabolical agency as exhibited at that examination. The occasion itself was mournful enough to draw forth these exclamations from one holding his opinions; and hence they are explained without a forced interpretation.   P.

Goody Proctor? A. Yes, here is Goody Cloyse. (Cloyse) When did I hurt thee? A. A great many times. (Cloyse) Oh, you are a grievous liar. Q. What did this Goody Cloyse do to you? A. She pinched and bit me till the blood came. Q. How long since this woman came and hurt you? A. Yesterday at meeting. Q. At any time before? A. Yes, a great many times.

Mary Walcot, who hurts you? A. Goody Cloyse. Q. What did she do to you? A. She hurt me. Q. Did she bring the book? A. Yes. Q. What were you to do with it? A. To touch it, and I should be well.— Then she fell into a fit. Q. Doth she come alone? A. Sometimes alone, and sometimes in company with Goody Nurse and Goody Corey, and a great many I do not know.—Then she fell into a fit again.

Abigail Williams, did you see a company at Mr. Parris's house eat and drink? A. Yes Sir, that was their sacrament. Q. How many were there? A. About forty, and Goody Cloyse and Goody Good were their deacons. Q. What was it? A. They said it was our blood, and they had it twice that day. Q. Mary Walcot, have you seen a white man? A. Yes Sir, a great many times. Q. What sort of a man was he? A. A fine grave man, and when he came, he made all the witches to tremble. Abigail Williams confirmed the same, and that they had such a sight at Deacon Ingersoll's. Q. Who was at Deacon Ingersoll's then? A. Goody Cloyse, Goody Nurse, Goody Corey, and Goody Good.

Then Sarah Cloyse asked for water, and sat down as one seized with a dying fainting fit; and several of the afflicted fell into fits, and some of them cried out, *Oh! her spirit is gone to prison to her sister Nurse.*

Elizabeth Proctor, you understand whereof you are charged, viz. to be guilty of sundry acts of witchcraft; what say you to it? Speak the truth. And so you that are afflicted, you must speak the truth, as you will answer it before God another day.

Mary Walcot, doth this woman hurt you? A. I never saw her so as to be hurt by her. Q. Mary Lewis, does she hurt you?—Her mouth was stopped. Q. Ann Putnam, does she hurt you?—She could not speak. Q. Abigail Williams, does she hurt you?—Her hand was thurst in her own mouth. Q. John (Indian), does this woman hurt you? A. This is the woman that came in her shift and choked me. Q. Did she ever bring the book? A. Yes Sir. Q. What to do? A. To write. Q. What, this woman? A. Yes Sir. Q. Are you sure of it? A. Yes Sir.

Again, Abigail Williams and Ann Putnam were spoke to by the court, but neither of them could make any answer, by reason of dumbness or other fits.

What do you say, Goody Proctor, to these things? A. I take God in heaven to be my witness, that I know nothing of it, no more than the child unborn. Q. Ann Putnam, doth this woman hurt you? A. Yes Sir, a great many times.

4*

Then the accused looked upon them and they fell into fits. Q. She does not bring the book to you, does she? A. Yes Sir, often, and saith she hath made her maid to set her hand to it. Q. Abigail Williams, does this woman hurt you? A. Yes Sir, often. Q. Does she bring the book to you? A. Yes. Q. What would she have you do with it? A. To write in it and I shall be well. Did not you, said Abigail, tell me, that your maid[40] had written? (Proctor) Dear child, it is not so. There is another judgment, dear child. Then Abigail and Ann had fits. By-and-by they cried out, *Look you, there is Goody Proctor upon the beam.* By-and-by both of them cried out of Goodman Proctor himself, and said he was a wizard. Immediately many, if not all of the bewitched had grievous fits.

Ann Putman, who hurt these? A. Goodman Proctor and his wife too. Afterwards, some of the afflicted cried: *There is Proctor going to take up Mrs. Pope's feet;* and her feet were immediately taken up. Q. What do you say, Goodman Proctor, to these things? A. I know not. I am innocent. Abigail Williams cried out, *There is Goodman Proctor going to Mrs. Pope,* and immediately said Pope fell into a fit. You see the Devil will deceive you; the children could see what you was going to do before the woman was hurt. I would advise you to repentance, for the Devil is about bringing you out.

Abigail Williams cried out again, *There is Goodman Proctor going to hurt Goody Bibber;* and immediately Goody Bibber fell into a fit. There was the like of Mary Walcot, and divers others.

Benjamin Gould gave in his testimony, that he had seen Goodman Corey and his wife, Proctor and his wife, Goody Cloyse, Goody Nurse, and Goody Griggs in his chamber last Thursday night. Elizabeth Hubbard was in a trance during the whole examination. During the examination of Elizabeth Proctor, Abigail Williams and Ann Putnam both made offer to strike at said Proctor; but when Abigail's hand came near, it opened, whereas it was made up into a fist before, and came down exceeding lightly as it drew near to said Proctor, and at length with open and extended fingers touched Proctor's hood very lightly. Immediately Abigail cried out, *her fingers, her fingers, her fingers burned,* and Ann Putman took on most grievously of her head, and sunk down.[41]

[40] The maid here alluded to was Mary Warren, one of the most violent of the accusing girls. She was a domestic in Proctor's family.   P.
[41] The documents which Gov. Hutchinson printed belong with the court files at Salem, which have been very carefully arranged and mounted by Mr. William P. Upham. These papers, or such of them as remain, were printed (with many errors) by Mr. W. E. Woodward, in *Records of Salem Witchcraft*, Roxbury, 1865, 2 vols. sm. 4to. Among these the papers which Gov. Hutchinson printed do not appear. They were doubtless borrowed by him, and never returned. In the Massachusetts archives is a volume of witchcraft papers (vol. cxxxv.), but these documents are not among them.
In 1860, Mr. N. I. Bowditch presented a collection of original papers relating to Salem witchcraft, which once belonged to the Salem court files, to the Massachusetts Historical Society. More than sixty years ago these papers came into possession of the late

Salem, April 11*th*, 1692.   Mr. Samuel Parris was desired by the honourable Thomas Danforth deputy governor, and the council, to take in writing the aforesaid examinations, and accordingly took and delivered them in ; and upon hearing the same, and seeing what was then seen, together with the charge of the afflicted persons, were by the advice of the Council all committed by us.

John Hathorne,   } Assistants.
Jonathan Corwin,   }

Facts often appear in their true light in after ages which had been seen in a false one by such as were upon the stage in the time of them. A strong bias is now evidently seen in favor of the accusers, and no measures were taken to discover the fraud. The same prejudice will appear through the whole process.

John the Indian, one of these accusers, was husband to Tituba the first witch complained of. She confessed and was committed to prison. Her husband, no doubt, was convinced he should stand a better chance among the afflicted than the accused. It is most probable some of the women acted from the same principle. As the afflicted increased, so did the accused, of course. Great pains were taken to bring some of them to confess ; but in general the accused persisted in their innocency until the prisons were filled. At length the friends of some of the accused urged them to a confession, although they knew they were innocent, the magistrates declaring that confessing was the way to obtain mercy. The first confession, which remains upon the files, is of Deliverance Hobbs, May 11th, 1692, being in prison. She owned everything she was required to do. The confessors, like the accusers, multiplied, the witches having always company with them, who were immediately sent for and examined. No wonder if they were affrighted to the last degree; they owned whatever their friends and magistrates would have them. Thus more than an hundred women, many of them of the most sober, virtuous livers, some of them of very reputable families in the towns of Salem, Beverly, Andover, Billerica, Newbury, were apprehended and examined, and generally committed, although most of them who confessed, after three or four months imprisonment, were admitted to bail. These confessions were all very much of the same tenor. One of them may serve as a specimen.

8th Sept. '92.   The examination and confession of Mary Osgood, wife

<hr>

Hon. John Pickering; who, says Mr. Bowditch, "as he was a sworn officer of the court, "had some scruples of conscience about retaining them himself; and therefore, after ex- "amining them, gave them to my late father [Dr. Nathaniel Bowditch].   (Proceedings, "1860-62, p. 31)."   The collection has been arranged and elegantly bound at the expense of Mr. Bowditch. The volume does not contain the papers printed by Gov. Hutchinson. As Gov. Hutchinson printed only portions of these papers, and doubtless took others which he did not print, it is a matter of some historical interest to know the present location (if they exist) of the original papers which he used.   P.

of Capt. Osgood, of Andover, taken before John Hathorne, Esq. and other their Majesty's justices.

She confesses, that about eleven years ago, when she was in a melancholy state and condition, she used to walk abroad in her orchard, and, upon a certain time, she saw the appearance of a cat at the end of the house, which yet she thought was a real cat. However, at that time it diverted her from praying to God, and instead thereof she prayed to the Devil; about which time she made a covenant with the Devil, who, as a black man, came to her and presented her a book, upon which she laid her finger and that left a red spot. And that upon her signing her book the devil told her he was her god, and that she should serve and worship him, and believes she consented to it. She says further, that about two years agone, she was carried through the air, in company with Deacon Frye's wife, Ebenezer Baker's wife, and Goody Tyler, to five-mile pond, where she was baptized by the Devil, who dipped her face in the water, and made her renounce her former baptism, and told her that she must be his, soul and body, forever, and that she must serve him, which she promised to do. She says, the renouncing her first baptism was after her dipping, and that she was transported back again through the air, in company with the fore-named persons, in the same manner as she went, and believes they were carried upon a pole. Q. How many persons were upon the pole? A. As I said before, viz. four persons and no more but whom she had named above. She confesses she has afflicted three persons, viz. John Sawdy, Martha Sprague and Rose Foster, and that she did it by pinching her bed clothes, and giving consent the Devil should do it in her shape, and that the Devil could not do it without her consent. She confesses the afflicting persons in the court, by the glance of her eye. She says, as she was coming down to Salem to be examined, she and the rest of the company with her stopped at Mr. Phillips's to refresh themselves; and the afflicted persons, being behind them upon the road, came up just as she was mounting again, and were then afflicted, and cried out upon her, so that she was forced to stay until they were all passed; and said she only looked that way towards them.

Do you know the devil can* take the shape of an innocent person and afflict? A I believe he cannot? Q. Who taught you this way of witchcraft? A. Satan, and that he promised her abundance of satisfaction and quietness in her future state, but never performed any thing; and that she has lived more miserably and more discontented since than ever before. She confesses further, that she herself, in company with Goody Parker, Goody Tyler and Goody Dean, had a meeting at Moses Tyler's house, last Monday night, to afflict, and that she and Goody Dean carried the shape of Mr. Dean, the minister, between them, to make persons believe that Mr.

---

* It is *can* in the examination, but, I suppose, by the answer, should have been wrote *can't.*   II.

Dean afflicted.   Q. What hindered you from accomplishing what you intended ?   A. The Lord would not suffer it so to be, that the devil should afflict in an innocent person's shape.   Q. Have you been at any other witch meeting ?   A. I know nothing thereof, as I shall answer in the presence of God and his people ; but said that the black man stood before her, and told her, that what she had confessed was a lie ; notwithstanding, she said that what she had confessed was true, and thereto put her hand.   Her husband being present, was asked if he judged his wife to be any way discomposed. He answered, that having lived with her so long, he doth not judge her to be any wise discomposed, but has cause to believe that what she has said is true.

When Mistress Osgood was first called, she afflicted Martha Sprague and Rose Foster by the glance of her eyes, and recovered them out of their fits by the touch of her hand.   Mary Lacey and Betty Johnson and Hannah Post saw Mistress Osgood afflicting Sprague and Foster.   The said Hannah Post and Mary Lacey and Betty Johnson, jun. and Rose Foster and Mary Richardson were afflicted by Mistress Osgood, in the time of her examination, and recovered by her touching of their hands.

" I underwritten, being appointed by authority to take this examination, do testify upon oath, taken in court, that this is a true copy of the substance of it, to the best of my knowledge, 5th Jan. 1692–3.   The within Mary Osgood was examined before their Majesties' justices of peace in Salem.   Attest.   John Higginson, Just. Peace."

Owned before the Grand Jury 5 Jan. 1692–3.   Robert Payne, Foreman."

Mr. Hale, who had the character of an impartial relator, acknowledges that the confessors generally went off from their confessions ; some saying " they remembered nothing of what they had said," others said " they had belied themselves," and yet he thinks, if the times had been calm, the condition of the confessors might have called for a *melius inquirendum ;* and seems to think remarkable daughters and granddaughters confirming their mother's and grandmothers' confession, and instances in the case of Goody Foster, her daughter Mary Lacey, and granddaughter Mary Lacey, jun.   Their confessions happen to be preserved, and a few extracts from them will show there was no need of further inquiries.[*]

21st July, '92.   Before Major Gedney, Mr. Hathorne, Mr. Corwin and Capt. Higginson.

Goody Foster, you remember we have three times spoken with you, and do you now remember what you then confessed to us?   Her former confession was read, which she owned to be all true.

---

[*] Mr. Perkins mentions eight or ten proofs of witchcraft, two only of which he supposes sufficient, viz. : the testimony of two witnesses and the confession of the party.   This authority probably had weight with the court as well as with Mr. Hale ; but Perkins says it is objected to the latter that a confession may be urged by force or threatening, &c., or by a persuasion that it is the best course to save life or obtain liberty.   H.

You have been engaged in very great wickedness, and some have been left to hardness of heart to deny; but it seems that God will give you more favor than others, inasmuch as you relent. But your daughter here hath confessed some things that you did not tell us of. Your daughter was with you and Goody Carrier, when you did ride upon the stick. A. I did not know it. Q. How long have you known your daughter to be engaged? A. I cannot tell, nor have I any knowledge of it at all. Q. Did you see your daughter at the meeting? A. No. Q. Did not you know your daughter to be a witch? A. No. Q. Your daughter said she was at the witches meeting, and that you yourself stood at a distance off and did not partake at that meeting; and you yourself said so also; give us a relation from the beginning until now. A. I know none of their names that were there, but only Goody Carrier. Q. Would you know their faces if you saw them? A. I cannot tell. Q. Were there not two companies in the field at the same time? A. I remember no more.

Mary Warren, one of the afflicted, said that Goody Carrier's shape told her, that this Goody Foster had made her daughter a witch. Q. Do not you acknowledge that you did so about thirteen years ago? A. No, and I know no more of my daughter's being a witch than what day I shall die upon. Q. Are you willing your daughter should make a full and free confession? A. Yes. Q. Are you willing to do so too? A. Yes. Q. You cannot expect peace of conscience without a free confession. A. If I knew any thing more, I would speak it to the utmost. Goody Lacey, the daughter, called in, began thus; Oh, mother! how do you do? We have left Christ, and the Devil hath gat hold of us. How shall I get rid of this evil one? I desire God to break my rocky heart that I may get the victory this time. Q. Goody Foster, you cannot get rid of this snare, your heart and mouth is not open. A. I did not see the Devil, I was praying to the Lord. Q. What Lord? A. To God. Q. What God do witches pray to? A. I cannot tell, the Lord help me. Q. Goody Lacey, had you no discourse with your mother in your riding? A. No, I think I had not a word. Q. Who rid foremost on that stick to the village? A. I suppose my mother. Goody Foster said that Goody Carrier was foremost. Q. Goody Lacey, how many years ago since they were baptized? A. Three or four years ago, I suppose. Q. Who baptized them? A. The old serpent. Q. How did he do it? A. He dipped their heads in the water, saying they were his, and that he had power over them. Q. Where was this? A. At Fall's river. Q. How many were baptized that day? A. Some of the chief; I think there were six baptized. Q. Name them. A. I think they were of the higher powers. These were then removed.

Mary Lacey, the grand-daughter, was brought in, and Mary Warren in a violent fit. Q. How dare you come in here, and bring the Devil with you, to afflict these poor creatures? A. I know nothing of it. Lacey laying her hand on Warren's arm; she recovered from her fit. Q. You are here accused for practising witchcraft upon Goody Ballard; which way do you do it? A. I cannot tell. Where is my mother that made me a witch, and I knew it not? Q. Can you look upon that maid, Mary Warren, and not hurt her? Look upon her in a friendly way. She trying so to do, struck her down with her eyes. Q. Do you acknowledge now you are a witch? A. Yes. Q. How long have you been a witch? A. Not above a week. Q. Did the Devil appear to you? A. Yes. Q. In what shape? A. In the shape of a horse. Q. What did he say to you? A. He bid me not to be afraid of any thing, and he would not bring me out; but he has proved a liar from the beginning. Q. When was this? A. I know not; above a week. Q. Did you set your hand to the book? A. No. Q. Did he bid you worship him? A. Yes; he bid me also afflict persons. You are now in the way to obtain mercy if you will confess and repent. She said, The Lord help me. Q. Do not you desire to be saved by Christ? A. Yes. Then you must confess freely what you know in this matter. She then proceeded. I was in bed, and the Devil came to me, and bid me obey him and I should want for nothing, and he would not bring me out. Q. But how long ago? A. A little more than a year. Q. Was that the first time? A. Yes. Q. How long was you gone from your father, when you run away? A. Two days. Q. Where had you your food? A. At John Stone's. Q. Did the Devil appear to you then, when you was abroad? A. No, but he put such thoughts in my mind as not to obey my parents. Q. Who did the Devil bid you afflict? A. Timothy Swan. Richard Carrier comes often a-nights and has me to afflict persons. Q. Where do ye go? A. To Goody Ballard's sometimes. Q. How many of you were there at a time? A. Richard Carrier and his mother, and my mother and grandmother. Upon reading over the confession so far, Goody Lacey, the mother, owned this last particular. Q. How many more witches are there in Andover? A. I know no more, but Richard Carrier.

Tell all the truth. A. I cannot yet. Q. Did you use at any time to ride upon a stick or pole? A. Yes. Q. How high? A. Sometimes above the trees. Q. Your mother struck down these afflicted persons, and she confessed so far, till at last she could shake hands with them freely and do them no hurt. Be you also free and tell the truth. What sort of worship did you do the Devil? A. He bid me pray to him and serve him and said he was a god and lord to me. Q. What meetings have you been at, at the village? A. I was once there and Richard Carrier rode with me on a pole, and the Devil carried us. Q. Did not some speak to you to afflict the people there? A. Yes, the Devil. Q. Was there not a man also among you there? A. None but the Devil. Q. What shape was the Devil in then? A. He was a black man, and had a high crowned hat. Q. Your mother and your grandmother say there was a minister there. How many men did you see there? A. I saw none but Richard Carrier. Q. Did you see none else? A. There was a minister there, and I think he is now in prison. Q. Were there not

5*

two* ministers there? A. Cannot tell. Q. Was there not one Mr. Burroughs there? A. Yes.

The examination contains many pages more of the same sort of proceedings which I am tired of transcribing.   Mr. Hale mentions also the case of
Richard Carrier, who was a lad of 18 years, accusing his mother, one that
suffered. but this examination was managed just in the same way.   He denied every thing at first, but was drawn to confession of every thing that his
examiners required.

So seven or eight of the confessors are said to have witnessed against the
minister Burroughs, but I have seen many examinations wherein he is accused just like this of Lacey. Richard Carrier's runs thus : " We met in a
green, which was the minister's pasture—we were in two companies at last.
I think there was a few men with them.—I heard Sarah Good talk of a minister or two.—One of them was she that had been at the eastward ; his name
is Burroughs, and is a little man.—I remember not the other's name."

After these examinations, the reader will find no great difficulty in giving
credit to the recantations of the confessors when they apprehended themselves out of danger.   One or two may be sufficient.

" We whose names are underwritten, inhabitants of Andover ; when as
that horrible and tremendous judgment beginning at Salem village in the
year 1692, by some called witchcraft, first breaking forth at Mr. Paris's
house, several young persons, being seemingly afflicted, did accuse several persons for afflicting them, and many there believing it so to be, we being informed that, if a person was sick, the afflicted persons could tell what or who was
the cause of that sickness : Joseph Ballard, of Andover, his wife being sick
at the same time, he either from himself or by the advice of others, fetched
two of the persons, called the afflicted persons, from Salem village to Andover, which was the beginning of that dreadful calamity that befel us in
Andover, believing the said accusations to be true, sent for the said persons to
come together to the meeting house in Andover, the afflicted persons being
there.   After Mr. Barnard had been at prayer, we were blindfolded, and
our hands were laid upon the afflicted persons, they being in their fits and
falling into their fits at our coming into their presence, as they said ; and
some led us and laid our hands upon them, and then they said they were
well, and that we were guilty of afflicting of them ; whereupon we were all
seized, as prisoners, by a warrant from the justice of the peace, and forthwith

* [Note in final draft.]   Mr. Deane, one of the ministers of Andover, then near four-
score, seems to have been in danger.   He is tenderly touched in several of the examinations, which might be owing to a fair character, and he may be one of the persons accused,
who caused a discouragement to further prosecutions.   "Deliverance Deane being asked
why she and the rest brought in Mr. Deane as afflicting persons, she answered, it was
Satan's subtilty, for he told her he would put a sham upon all these things, and make people believe that he did afflict.   She said Mrs. Osgood and she gave their consent the devil
should bring Mr. Deane's shape to afflict.   Being asked again if Mrs. Osgood and she acted
this business, she said yes."   Mr. Deane was much beholden to this woman.   H.

carried to Salem. And by reason of that sudden surprisal, we knowing ourselves altogether innocent of that crime, we were all exceedingly astonished and amazed, and consternated and affrighted even out of our reason ; and our nearest and dearest relations, seeing us in that dreadful condition, and knowing our great danger, apprehending that there was no other way to save our lives, as the case was then circumstanced, but by our confessing ourselves to be such and such persons as the afflicted represented us to be, they, out of tender love and pity, persuaded us to confess what we did confess. And indeed that confession, that it is said we made, was no other than what was suggested to us by some gentlemen, they telling us that we were witches, and they knew it, and we knew it, and they knew that we knew it, which made us think that it was so ; and our understanding, our reason, our faculties almost gone, we were not capable of judging our condition ; as also the hard measures they used with us rendered us incapable of making our defence, but said any thing and every thing which they desired, and most of what we said was but in effect a consenting to what they said. Some time after, when we were better composed, they telling us of what we had confessed, we did profess that we were innocent and ignorant of such things ; and we hearing that Samuel Wardwell had renounced his confession, and quickly after condemned and executed, some of us were told that we were going after Wardwell.

> "Mary Osgood,   Deliverance Dane,   Sarah Wilson,
> Mary Tiler,   Abigail Barker,   Hannah Tiler."

These unhappy people were not only in the manner which has been related, brought to confession, but also obliged to swear to the truth of it. At the Superior Court in January they all abode by their confessions. They could not tell what the disposition of the court and juries would be, and the temptation was the same as at the first examination. But there was one Margaret Jacobs, who had more courage than the rest. She had been brought not only to accuse herself, but Mr. Burroughs, the minister, and even her own grandfather. Before their execution, she was struck with horror, and begged forgiveness of Burroughs, who readily forgave her, and prayed with her, and for her. An imposthume in her head prevented her trial at the court of Oyer and Terminer. At the Superior Court in January she delivered a writing in the words following :—

"The humble declaration of Margaret Jacobs unto the honoured court now sitting at Salem, sheweth,

"That whereas your poor and humble declarant being closely confined here in Salem jail for the crime of witchcraft, which crime, thanks be to the Lord, I am altogether ignorant of, as will appear at the great day of judgment. May it please the honoured court, I was cried out upon by some of the possessed persons, as afflicting of them ; whereupon I was brought to my examination, which persons at the sight of me fell down, which did very much startle and affright me. The Lord above knows I knew nothing, in the least measure, how or who afflicted them ; they told me, without doubt I did, or else they would not fall down at me ; they told me if I would not confess, I should be put down into the dungeon and would be hanged, but if I would confess I should have my life; the which did so affright me, with my own vile wicked heart, to save my life made me make the confession I did, which confession, may it please the honoured court, is altogether false and untrue.   The very first night after I had made my confession, I was in such horror of conscience that I could not sleep, for fear the Devil should carry me away for telling such horrid lies. I was, may it please the honoured court, sworn to my confession, as I understand since, but then, at that time, was ignorant of it, not knowing what an oath did mean. The Lord, I hope, in whom I trust, out of the abundance of his mercy, will forgive me my false forswearing myself. What I said was altogether false, against my grandfather, and Mr. Burroughs, which I did to save my life and to have my liberty ; but the Lord, charging it to my conscience made me in so much horror, that I could not contain myself before I had denied my confession, which I did, though I saw nothing but death before me, choosing rather death with a quiet conscience, than to live in such horror, which I could not suffer.   Whereupon my denying my confession, I was committed to close prison, where I have enjoyed more felicity in spirit a thousand times than I did before in my enlargement.

"And now, may it please your honours, your poor and humble declarant having, in part, given your honours a description of my condition, do leave it to your honours pious and judicious discretions to take pity and compassion on my young and tender years ; to act and do with me as the Lord above and your honours shall see good, having no friend but the Lord to plead my cause for me ; not being guilty in the least measure of the crime of witchcraft, nor any other sin that deserves death from man ; and your poor and humble declarant shall forever pray, as she is bound in duty, for your honours' happiness in this life, and eternal felicity in the world to come. So prays your honours declarant.   Margaret Jacobs."

I shall now proceed in the relation of facts. The accusers having charged a great number in the county of Essex, I find in the examinations frequent mention of strangers whose shapes or specters were unknown to the afflicted, and now and then the names of a person at Boston and other distant places. Several some time after mention Mr. Dean, one of the ministers of Andover, but touch him more tenderly, somewhat as Mrs. Osgood in her confession, than they do Burroughs. Mr. Dean probably was better known and esteemed than the other, or he would have stood a bad chance.

Mr. Nathaniel Cary,[42] a gentleman of figure in the town of Charlestown,

[42] Mr. Cary's account is in Calef, pp. 95-99.
All my references to C. Mather's *Wonders of the Invisible World*, and to Calef, are to the London editions of 1693 and 1700. Mr. S. G. Drake reprints both works in his *Witchcraft Delusion in New England* (Roxbury, 1866, 3 vols. sm. 4to), with the original paging. This

hearing that some at Salem had complained of his wife for afflicting them, they went to Salem together out of curiosity to see whether the afflicted knew her. They happened to arrive just as the justices were going into the meeting house, where they held the court, to examine prisoners. All that were brought in were accused, and the girls fell into fits as usual, but no notice was taken of Mrs. Cary except that one or two of the afflicted came to her and asked her name. After the examination her husband went into a tavern, having encouragement that he should have an opportunity of discoursing with the girl who had accused his wife. There he met with John the afflicted Indian, who attended as a servant in the house. He had been there but a short time before the girls came in and tumbled about the floor, and cried out *Cary*, and a warrant from the justices was immediately sent to apprehend her. Two of the girls accused her, neither of whom she had ever heard of before, and soon after the Indian joined them. The justices, by her husband's account, used her very roughly, and it was to no purpose to make any defence or to offer any bail, but she was committed to prison in Boston and removed from thence by *habeas corpus* to Cambridge and there laid in irons. When the trials at Salem came on her husband went there, and finding how things were managed, thought it high time to contrive her escape. They fled to New-York, where Gov. Fletcher received them courteously. They petitioned for a trial in the county where they lived. If the judges supposed it necessary to try the offence where it was committed, her body being in Middlesex and her specter in Essex, it is probable they were under doubt.

About a week after, viz. the latter end of May, some of the afflicted accused Capt. John Alden,[43] of Boston. He had been many years master of a sloop in the country service employed between Boston and the eastern country, to supply the garrisons, &c.; and the justices allowed had always had the character of an honest man, though one of them, Gedney, told him at his examination he then saw cause to think otherwise. Alden, in the account he gives, says that the accuser pointed first to another man and said nothing, but that upon the man who held her his stooping down to her ear, she cried out *Alden, Alden,* &c. All were ordered into the street and a ring made, and then she cried out, *There stands Alden, a bold fellow with his hat on, sells powder and shot to the Indians, lies with the squaws and has papooses.* He was immediately taken into custody of the marshal [George

is the best reprint of these noted books. An excellent and inexpensive edition of the " *Wonders* " appeared in J. Russell Smith's *Library of Old Authors* (London, 1862, 16mo.), in which the original paging is not indicated. This edition is especially desirable as it contains reprints of *A Further Account of the Tryals of the New England Witches*, 1693, and *Cases of Conscience concerning Evil Spirits personating Men*, 1693, both by Increase Mather. There are several other reprints of the *Wonders* and of Calef's *More Wonders*; but they are carelessly done, and are not reliable for historical purposes. A copy (with one leaf missing) of the original *Wonders* (Boston, 1693), brought two hundred and ninety dollars at the Woodward auction sale in New-York, April 19, 1869. P.

[43] See Calef, pp. 98-100. P.

6

Herrick] and required to deliver up his sword. A further examination was had in the meeting house, his hands held open by the officer that he might not pinch the afflicted, and upon their being struck down at the sight of him and making their usual cries he was committed to the jail in Boston, where he lay fifteen weeks, and then was prevailed on by his friends to make his escape, and to absent himself until the consternation of the people was a little abated, and they had recovered their senses.

By this time about one hundred persons were in the several prisons[44] charged with witchcraft. The court of Oyer and Terminer began at Salem the first week in June [June 2d]. Only one of the accused, viz. Bridget Bishop,[45] alias Oliver, was brought upon trial. She had been charged with witchcraft twenty years before, by a person who acknowledged his guilt in accusing her upon his death-bed; but being a fractious old woman the losses the neighbors met with in their cattle and poultry, or by oversetting their carts, &c., were ascribed to her, and now given in evidence. This, together with the hearsay from the specters sworn to in court by the afflicted and confessing confederates, and an excrescence found some where upon her which was called a teat, was thought by court and jury plenary proof, and she was convicted, and on the 10th of June executed.

The court adjourned to the 30th of June, and in the mean time the Governor and Council desired the opinion of several ministers upon the state of things as they then stood, which was given as follows:—

"The return of several ministers consulted by his excellency and the honourable council upon the present witchcraft in Salem village.

Boston, June 15th, 1692.

"1. The afflicted state of our poor neighbours, that are now suffering by molestations from the invisible world, we apprehend so deplorable, that we think their condition calls for the utmost help of all persons in their several capacities.

[44] The jails of Boston and Ipswich were filled, as well as that of Salem. Many of the accused were heads of families; the season for putting in crops was far advanced, and farm labor had been interrupted. "Upon consideration," say the records of the Council for May 27, 1692, "that there are many criminal offenders now in custody, some whereof "have lain long, and many inconveniencies attending the thronging of the goals at this hot "season of the year, there being no judicatories or courts of justice yet established: Or- "dered, That a special commission of Oyer and Terminer be made out to William "Stoughton, John Richards, Nathaniel Saltonstall, Wait Winthrop, Bartholomew Gedney, "Samuel Sewall, John Hathorne, Jonathan Corwin and Peter Sergeant, Esquires, assign- "ing them to be justices, or any five of them (whereof William Stoughton, John Richards "and Bartholomew Gedney Esq's to be one), to inquire of, hear and determine for this "time, according to the law and custom of England and of this their Magesties' Province, all "and all manner of crimes and offences had, made, done or perpetrated within the coun- "ties of Suffolk, Essex, Middlesex, and each of them." Capt. Stephen Sewall was ap- pointed clerk, and Thomas Newton as attorney. George Corwin was the sheriff, and Geo. Herrick, marshal.   P.
[45] The testimony and other papers, in the case of Bridget Bishop, are in *Records of Salem Witchcraft*, Vol. i. pp. 135-172; *Wonders of the Invisible World*, pp. 65-70; and Calef's *More Wonders*, pp. 119-126.   P.

" 2. We cannot but, with all thankfulness, acknowledge the success which the merciful God has given unto the sedulous and assiduous endeavours of our honourable rulers, to detect the abominable witchcrafts which have been committed in the country, humbly praying, that the discovery of those mysterious and mischievous wickednesses may be perfected.

" 3. We judge that, in the prosecution of these and all such witchcrafts, there is need of a very critical and exquisite caution, lest by too much credulity for things received only upon the Devil's authority, there be a door opened for a long train of miserable consequences, and Satan get an advantage over us ; for we should not be ignorant of his devices.

" 4. As in complaints upon witchcrafts, there may be matters of inquiry which do not amount unto matters of presumption, and there may be matters of presumption which yet may not be matters of conviction, so it is necessary, that all proceedings thereabout be managed with an exceeding tenderness towards those that may be complained of, especially if they have been persons formerly of an unblemished reputation.

" 5. When the first inquiry is made into the circumstances of such as may lie under the just suspicion of witchcrafts, we could wish that there may be admitted as little as is possible of such noise, company and openness as may too hastily expose them that are examined, and that there may no thing be used as a test for the trial of the suspected, the lawfulness whereof may be doubted among the people of God ; but that the directions given by such judicious writers as Perkins and Bernard [be consulted in such a case].

" 6. Presumptions whereupon persons may be committed, and, much more, convictions whereupon persons may be condemned as guilty of witchcrafts, ought certainly to be more considerable than barely the accused person's being represented by a specter unto the afflicted ; inasmuch as it is an undoubted and notorious thing, that a demon may, by God's permission, appear, even to ill purposes, in the shape of an innocent, yea, and a virtuous man. Nor can we esteem alterations made in the sufferers, by a look or touch of the accused, to be an infallible evidence of guilt, but frequently liable to be abused by the Devil's legerdemains.

" 7. We know not whether some remarkable affronts given to the Devils by our disbelieving those testimonies whose whole force and strength is from them alone, may not put a period unto the progress of the dreadful calamity begun upon us, in the accusations of so many persons, whereof some, we hope, are yet clear from the great transgression laid unto their charge.

" 8. Nevertheless, we cannot but humbly recommend unto the government, the speedy and vigorous prosecution of such as have rendered themselves obnoxious, according to the direction given in the laws of God, and the wholesome statutes of the English nation, for the detection of witchcrafts."[46]

[46] Gov. Hutchinson found this document in the Postscript of Increase Mather's *Cases of Conscience*, 1693. His copy, in the early draft, is quite correct, except that the concluding words of the fifth section " be consulted in such a case " were accidentally omitted. In

6*

The two first and the last sections of this advice took away the force of all the others, and the prosecutions went on with more vigor than before. The exquisite caution in separating the evidence upon the Devil's authority from the rest, in the third section, and the disbelieving those testimonies whose whole force is from the Devil alone in the seventh section, must have puzzled the judges, and they had need of some further authorities to guide them than Perkins or Bernard,[47] or any other books they were furnished with.[48]

I was at a loss until I met with this return, by what law they proceeded. The old constitution was dissolved; no laws of the colony were in force, witchcraft is no offence by the common law of England. The statute of James I. was indeed more ancient than the colony charter, but no statute had ever been adopted here. The General Assembly had not then met, and there could have been no provision made by a Province law, but it seems by the eighth section that the English statutes were made the rule upon this extraordinary occasion. But what authority the court had to change the sentence from burning to hanging, I cannot conceive.[49] Before the other trials the law against witchcraft under the first charter was established with the other Colony laws. The authority by which the court sat may as well be called in question. No authority is given by the Province charter to any powers short of the whole General Court to constitute courts of justice. The Governor indeed, with the consent of the Council, appoints judges, commissioners of Oyer and Terminer, and all officers belonging to the courts. It is strange they did not tarry until the Assembly met. A judge shall not be punished for mere error of judgment, but it certainly

making his final draft he probably noticed that the sentence was incomplete, and instead of recurring to the original authority, supplied words of his own: "may be observed." This, and similar facts, show that he made little use of original authorities in preparing his final draft. In his last copy of this document, and in printing, ten errors were made in words and transpositions, but one of which appear in the early draft. The most important error was *defeat* for *detect* in the second section.

[47] Richard Bernard, 1566-1651, a famous Puritan minister at Batcomb in Somerset. His *Guide to Grand Jury-men in cases of Witchcraft* (London, 1627), says Increase Mather, "is a solid and wise treatise. As for the judgment of the elders in New-England, so far as "I can learn, they do generally concur with Mr. Perkins and Mr. Bernard." (*Cases of Conscience*, pp. 252-3, ed. 1862.)   P.

[48] Gov. Hutchinson omitted this paragraph when he prepared his next and final draft, which was a judicious proceeding. The above is a view of the document which may occur to a reader on a first and superficial examination; and it has been claimed by a late writer that "the paper is so worded as to mislead." The paper was drawn by Cotton Mather; and was "concurringly presented before his Excellency and Council by twelve ministers" of Boston and the vicinity. (*Cases of Conscience*, Postscript.) Those twelve men knew the meaning of language; and it is hardly possible to believe that they would concur, at that solemn period, in a series of recommendations to the public authorities which carried a contradiction, if not a fraud, on the face of the document. Hutchinson's omission of the passage may be regarded as a retraction of his first impressions, resulting from further investigation. The advice, in my opinion, is wholly consistent; but this is not the place to discuss the point. I purpose to do this on some other occasion.   P.

[49] This statement shows that Hutchinson had not seen the records of the Council, a copy of which was made in the British State Paper office in 1846, and is now in the office of the Secretary of the State of Massachusetts.   P.

behooves him, in a trial for life especially, to consider well by what authority he acts.

The court was held again by adjournment at Salem, June 30. Six [five] women were brought upon trial, Sarah Good, Rebecca Nurse, Susannah Martin, Elizabeth Howe, and Sarah Wildes.[50] The court and jury seemed to have had no difficulty with any but Nurse. She was a church member, and probably her good character caused the jury to bring in a verdict not guilty; but the accusers making a very great clamor and the court expressing their dissatisfaction with the verdict, the jury desired to go out again, and then brought her in guilty. The foreman of the jury gave the following certificate to satisfy her relations what induced an alteration of the verdict.

"July 4th, 1692.

"I Thomas Fisk, the subscriber hereof, being one of them that were of the jury the last week at Salem court, upon the trial of Rebekah Nurse, &c. being desired, by some of the relations, to give a reason why the jury brought her in *guilty*, after the verdict *not guilty;* I do hereby give my reasons to be as follows, viz.:

"When the verdict, *not guilty,* was [given], the honoured court was pleased to object against it, saying to them, that they think they let slip the words which the prisoner at the bar spake against herself, which were spoken in reply to Goodwife Hobbs and her daughter, who had been faulty in setting their hands to the Devil's book, as they had confessed formerly; the words were, 'What do these persons give in evidence against me now? they used to come among us?' After the honoured court had manifested their dissatisfaction of the verdict, several of the jury declared themselves desirous to go out again, and thereupon the honoured court gave leave; but when we came to consider the case, I could not tell how to take her words as an evidence against her, till she had a further opportunity to put her sense upon them, if she would take it; and then going into court, I mentioned the words aforesaid, which by one of the court were affirmed to have been spoken by her, she being then at the bar, but made no reply nor interpretation of them; whereupon, these words were to me a principal evidence against her. Thomas Fisk."

Nurse, being informed of the use which had been made of her words, gave in a declaration to the court, that "when she said Hobbs and her daughter were of her company, she meant no more than that they were prisoners as well as herself; and that, being hard of hearing, she did not know what the foreman of the jury said." But her declaration had no effect.

[50] Erroneously printed "Wilder." The trials of Susannah Martin and Elizabeth How are in *Records of Salem Witchcraft,* vol. i. 193-215, and vol. ii. pp. 69-93; Mather's *Wonders,* pp. 70-80, and, with the trials of Bishop, Burroughs and Carrier, were copied by Calef, pp. 114-139.   P.

The minister of Salem Mr. [Nicholas] Noyes was over zealous in these prosecutions. He excommunicated this honest old woman after her condemnation. One part of the form seems to have been unnecessary, delivering her over to Satan. He supposed she had delivered herself up to him long before. But her life and conversation had been such, of which many testimonies were given, that the remembrance of it, as soon as the people returned to the use of their reason, must have wiped off all the reproach which had been occasioned by the manner of her death.

Calef, who when he wrote was generally supposed to be under unreasonable prejudice against the country, which lessened the credit of his narrative, says that at the trial of Sarah Good, one of the afflicted fell into a fit, and after recovery cried out that the prisoner had stabbed her and broke the knife in doing it, and a piece of the knife was found upon the afflicted person; but a young man declared that the day before he broke that very knife and threw away a piece of it, this afflicted person being then present; and adds that the court bid her tell no more lies, but went on notwithstanding this fraud to improve her as a witness against other prisoners.* This account, if true, would give me a more unfavorable opinion even of the integrity of the court, if I had not met with something not unlike to it in the trials before Sir Matthew Hale. The afflicted children in their fits upon the least touch from Rose Cullender, one of the supposed witches, would shriek out, which they would not do when touched by any other person. Lest there should be any fraud, Lord Cornwallis, Sir Edmund Bacon, Sergeant Keeling and other gentlemen attended one of the girls whilst she was in her fits at another part of the hall, and one of the witches was brought, and an apron put before the girl's eyes, but instead of the witch's hand another person's hand was taken to touch the girl, who thereupon shrieked out as she used to do. The gentlemen returned and declared to the court they believed the whole was an imposture. The witch was found guilty notwithstanding, and the judge and all the court were fully satisfied with the verdict and awarded sentence accordingly.

Susannah Martin had been suspected, ever since 1669, so that a great number of witch stories were told of her, and many of them given in evidence. One of the other being told by the minister at the place of execution, that he knew she was a witch, and therefore advised her to confess, she replied that he lied, and that she was no more a witch than he was a wizard, and if he took away her life, God would give him blood to drink.

At one of these trials it is said that one of the accusers charged Mr. Willard, a minister of Boston, and that she was sent out of court, and afterwards a report spread that she was mistaken in the person.† It is more probable that she intended [John] Willard, who was then in prison, and that it was given out that the audience were mistaken.

At the next adjournment, Aug. 5th, George Burroughs, John Proctor

<hr/>

* Calef [p. 101].　　H.　　　　　　† Calef [p. 103].　　H.

and Elizabeth his wife, John Willard, George Jacobs and Martha Carrier were all found guilty, condemned, and all executed the 19th of August, except Elizabeth Proctor, who escaped by pleading her belly.

Burroughs had preached some years before, but it seems not to acceptance, at Salem village. Afterward he preached at Wells in the Province of Maine. As a specimen of the proceedings in all the trials we shall be a little more particular in relating his.

The indictment was as follows.

Anno Regis et Reginæ, &c. quarto.

Essex ss. The jurors for our sovereign lord and lady the king and queen present, that George Burroughs, late of Falmouth in the province of Massachusetts Bay, clerk, the ninth day of May, in the fourth year of the reign of our sovereign lord and lady William and Mary, by the grace of God of England, Scotland, France and Ireland, king and queen, defenders of the faith, &c. and divers other days and times, as well before as after, certain detestable arts called witchcrafts and sorceries, wickedly and feloniously hath used, practised and exercised, at and within the township of Salem, in the county of Essex aforesaid, in, upon and against one Mary Walcot, of Salem village, in the county of Essex, single woman; by which said wicked arts, the said Mary Walcot, the ninth day of May in the fourth year abovesaid, and divers other days and times as well before as after, was and is tortured, afflicted, pined, consumed, wasted and tormented, against the peace of our sovereign lord and lady the king and queen, and against the form of the statute in that case made and provided. Endorsed *Billa vera.* Three other bills were found for the like upon other persons, to all which he pleaded not guilty, and put himself upon trial, &c.

The afflicted and confessing witches were first examined, for although, by the advice of the elders, this kind of evidence was not to be deemed infallible; yet it was presumptive, and, with other circumstances, sufficient proof. It would be tedious to recite the whole of this evidence, especially as it was of the same sort with what has been already related in the confessions. The most material circumstance which distinguished him [Burroughs] from the rest, was, that he was to be a king in Satan's empire.

The other evidence was that being a little man he had performed feats beyond the strength of a giant; particularly that he would take a gun of seven feet barrel behind the lock and hold it out with one hand; that he would take up a barrel of molasses or cider and carry them in a disadvantageous place and posture from a canoe to the shore; and when in his vindication he urged that an Indian which was there held out the gun as he did, the witnesses not seeing or not remembering any Indian, it was supposed it must be the black man or the devil, who, the witnesses swore, looks like an Indian.

Besides this it was sworn that he had treated his wives, having been twice married, very harshly, and would pretend, when he had been absent from

7

home, that he could tell what had been said to them, and that he persuaded them to swear, and to oblige themselves by a writing, which in the printed account of the trial is called " a Covenant," not to reveal his secrets, and that they had privately complained to the neighbors that their house was haunted by spirits. One of his wife's brothers also swore that going out after strawberries they rode very softly—slowly, I suppose—two or three miles, when Burroughs went into the bushes, after which they rode back a quick pace, and when they came near home, to their astonishment found him on foot with them, and that he fell to chiding his wife for talking with her brother about him, and said he knew their thoughts, which his brother intimated was more than the Devil knew, but Burroughs replied his god told him.

The prisoner said, in his defence, a man was with him when his brother left him, which was also supposed to be the black man.

This was the sum of the evidence. He is said to have used many twistings and turnings, and to have contradicted himself in making his defence. At his execution he concluded his prayer with the Lord's prayer, probably to show his innocence, for it was generally received that a witch could not say the Lord's prayer, and it was used as a test at the examinations when several of the old women, as children often do, blundered at *give* and *forgive* in the fourth and fifth petitions, and it was improved against them.

September 9th, *Martha Corey, Mary Esty, Alice Parker, Ann Pudeator,* Dorcas Hoar and Mary Bradbury were tried; and Sept. 17 *Margaret Scott, Wilmot Read, Samuel Wardwell, Mary Parker,* Abigail Faulkner, Rebekah Eames, Mary Lacey, Ann Foster, Abigail Hobbs, and all received sentence of death. Those in italics were executed September 22d.

Mary Esty, who was sister to Nurse, put into the court a petition in which she tells them that, although she was conscious of her own innocence, yet she did not ask her own life, but prayed them before they condemned any more they would examine some of the confessing witches. who she knew had belied themselves and others, which she was sure would appear in the world to which she was going, if it did not in this world.

Those that were not executed probably confessed their guilt. All whose examinations remain on the files, of which there are three or four, did so. Wardwell had confessed. but recanted and suffered. His own wife, as well as his daughter, accused him and saved themselves. There are a great number of instances of children and parents accusing each other. I have met with no other than this of husbands or wives, and surely this one ought not to have been suffered.

Giles Corey was the only person, besides what have been named. who suffered death. He, seeing the fate of those who had put themselves upon trial, refused to plead to the indictment; but the judges who were not careful enough in observing the rules of law in favor of the prisoners, took care to do it against this unhappy man, and he was pressed to death; the only instance I have ever heard of in any of the English colonies.[51] History furnishes us perhaps with as many instances of cruelty proceeding from superstition, as from the most savage barbarous temper of mind.

Besides the irregularities which I have already mentioned in these trials, the court admitted evidence to be given of facts. not laid in the indictments, to prove witchcraft eight, ten or fifteen years before; indeed, no other sort of evidence was offered to prove facts in the indictments but the spectral evidence, which, in the opinion of the divines, was not sufficient. It would have been well if they had consulted lawyers[52] also, who would have told

[51] Samuel Sewall, one of the judges in the witchcraft trials, made, on this occasion, the following entry in his Diary—for the use of which I am indebted to the courtesy of the Massachusetts Historical Society: " Monday, Sept. 19, 1692. About noon, at Salem, Giles " Corey was pressed to death for standing mute; much pains was used with him two days, " one after another, by the court and Capt. Gardner of Nantucket, who had been his " acquaintance; but all in vain. Sept. 20. Now I hear from Salem, that about eighteen " years ago, he was suspected to have stamped and pressed a man to death; but was cleared. " 'Twas not remembered till Ann Putnam was told of it by said Corey's specter, the sab- " bath-day night before the execution."

The following touching relation of the sufferings of the Corey family during the year 1692, is in *Mass. Archives*, vol. cxxxv. fol. 161. For the purpose of preserving the quaintness of the original document, I have copied it *verbatim*.

" To the Honrable Commite Apointed by the Generall Court to make enquire with Res- " pect to the Suferings in The year 1692 &c
" these are to giue you a Short Acount of our Sorrows and Suferings which was in the yere " 1692 Some time in march our honerd father and mother Giles Corey & martha his wife " ware acused for Suposed wicheraft and imprisoned and ware Remoued from on prison to " another as from Salem to ipswitch & from ipswitch to boston and from boston to Salem " againe and soe remained in close imprisonment about four months we ware att the whole " Charge of their maintainance which was very chargable and soe much the more being soe " farr adistant from us as also by Reason of soe many remoues in all which we could doe not " less then Acompanie them which further added both to our trouble and Charge and al- " though that was very Great in the least of our greavence or cause of These lines but that " which breakes our harts and for which wee goe mourning still is that our father was put to " soe cruell a death as being prest to death our mother was put to death also though in " another way And we Cannot Sufficiantly exspress our Griffe for the loss of our father and " mother in such away Soe we Cannot Compute our exspences and coast but shall Comite " to your wisdome to iudge of but after our fathers death the Shirfe thretend to size our " fathers estate and for feare tharof we Complied with him and paid him eleauen pound six " shillings in monie by which we have bee[n] greaty damnified & impouerishd by being ex- " sposed to sell Creaturs and other things for litle more then half the worth of them to get the " monie to pay as aforesed and to maintain our father & mother in prison but that which is " grieueous to us is that wee are not only impouerished but also Reproached and soe may bee " for all generatians and that wrongfully tow unless something bee done fore the remoueall " thearof all which we humbly Committe to the honarable Court Praying God to direct to " that which may be axceptable in his Sight and for the good of this land

" September the 13th 1710   Wee Subscrib your humbl Scaruants in all
                                                " Christian obedeance
" We Cannot Judge our necessary Expense   JOHN MOULTON who mared Elizabeth Corey
" to be less than Ten pounds   daughtr of the abovesd in the behalf of the
                                                " reast of that familie "   v.

[52] The author has already stated that the court chiefly relied on the decisions of Sir Matthew Hale, and " the authorities of Keble, Dalton and other lawyers of note who lay down " rules of conviction as absurd as any ever adopted in New-England." These illegal methods of procedure the judges certainly did not receive from the clergy, or from Perkins and Bernard, the clerical authorities recommended to them. Lord Campbell brings similar charges against Sir Matthew Hale, in connection with the Bury St. Edmund's trial. He

7*

them that evidence ought not to be admitted even against the general character of persons charged criminally unless they offer evidence in favor of it, much less ought their whole lives to be arraigned and no opportunity given them of making defence.

This court of Oyer and Terminer, happily for the country, sat no more. Nineteen persons had been executed; but the eyes of the country in general were not yet opened. The prison at Salem was so full that some were obliged to be removed, and many were in other prisons reserved for trial. The General Court which sat in October, although they had revived the old colony law which was in these words, "If any man or woman be a witch, that is, hath or consulteth with a familiar spirit, they shall be put to death"—yet this not being explicit enough, they enacted another in the words of the statute of King James, which continued in force until the trials were over, but both were afterwards disallowed by the crown.[53] Another act was passed, constituting a Supreme Court,[54] which was to be held at Salem in January; but before that time many who had been forward in these prosecutions became sensible of their error. Time for consideration seems to be reason enough to be assigned for it; but another reason has been given. Ordinarily persons of the lowest rank, the dregs of the people, have had the misfortune of being charged with witchcraft; and although this was the case in many instances here, yet there were a number of women of as reputable families as any in the towns where they lived, who were charged and imprisoned, and several persons of still superior rank were hinted at by the pretended bewitched or the confessing

says, " he violated the plainest rules of justice, and really was the murderer of two inno-
" cent women. . . . . . I would very readily have pardoned him for an undoubted belief in
" witchcraft, and I should have considered that this belief detracted little from his charac-
" ter for discernment and humanity. . . . . . There not only was no evidence against them
" which ought to have weighed in the mind of any reasonable man who believed in witch-
" craft; but during the trial the imposture practised by the prosecutors was detected and
" exposed. The enormous violation of justice then perpetrated has become more revolting
" as the mists of ignorance, which partly covered it, have been dispersed." (*Lives of the
Chief Justices*, vol. i. p. 561, 563.)   P.

[53] The colony law against witchcraft was re-enacted October 29, 1692. The statute of King James I. was passed December 14, and published two days later. Both were disallowed by the Privy Council, Aug. 22, 1695; the latter for " being not found to agree with the statute " of King James I., whereby the dower is saved to the widow, and the inheritance to the " heir of the party convicted." (*Province Laws*, 1869, vol. i. pp. 55, 91.)   P.

[54] The law was passed Nov. 25. December 7, William Stoughton was elected chief justice (receiving every vote present), and Thomas Danforth, John Richards, Wait Winthrop and Samuel Sewall, receiving only majorities as associate judges. December 22, they received their commissions.

Gov. Hutchinson states that the colony law against witchcraft was revived by the first act of the Provincial Assembly, passed June 15, and published June 28, 1692, providing " That all the local laws of Massachusetts Bay and New Plymouth, being not repugnant to " the laws of England, do remain in full force, until the 10 day of November next." As the charges alleged in the witchcraft trials were committed, and proceedings instituted, before June 28, and the special court was instructed, May 27, to proceed under English law and custom, it is probable that the court tried and executed every one of its victims under English law, the statute of James I. Trials were held after the old colony law was re-enacted; but no persons were executed after September 22, 1692.   P.

witches. The latter had no other way of saving themselves. Some of the
persons were publicly named. Dudley Bradstreet, a justice of the peace,
who had been appointed one of President Dudley's council, thought it necessary to abscond; so did his brother John Bradstreet, sons of the late Governor Bradstreet. Calef says it was intimated that Sir William Phips's lady
was accused.[55] One at Boston complained of being afflicted by the secretary
of Connecticut colony.*

At the Superior Court held at Salem in January, the grand jury found
bills against about fifty persons, all but one or two women, who either were
in prison, or under bonds for their appearance. They were all but three
acquitted by the petty jury, and those three were pardoned by the Governor. Divers others were brought upon trial soon after at Charlestown in
the county of Middlesex, and all acquitted. The juries changed sooner
than the judges. The opinion which the latter had of their own superior
understanding and judgment probably made them more backward in own-
ing or discovering their errors. One of them, however, Mr. Sewall, who
always had the character of great integrity, at a public fast sometime after
gave in a bill, or note, to the minister, acknowledging his errors and desiring to humble himself in the sight of God and his people, and stood up
while the note was reading.[56] It is said that the chief justice Mr. Stough-

---

[55] Nathaniel Saltonstall, of Haverhill, was also under suspicion. Judge Sewall, March
3, 1692-3, wrote to him a letter expressing disbelief in such reports, and sympathy for him
and his family. The letter is in Judge Sewall's Diary under that date. P.

* "As to what you mention, concerning that poor creature in your town that is afflicted,
and mentioned my name to yourself and son, I return you hearty thanks for your intima-
tion about it, and for your charity therein mentioned; and I have great cause to bless God,
who, of his mercy hitherto, hath not left me to fall into such an horrid evil." *Extract from
letter [of Secretary Allen] to I. Mather, Hartford*, 18 *March*, 92 [-3]. H.

[56] It is singular that Gov. Hutchinson did not give the date of this confession, which is
noted in Calef. In this manuscript he says, "sometime after." In the final draft he says,
"it was not long before one of the judges was sensible of his error." The confession was
made January 14, 1696-7, nearly five years after the error was committed to which
he alludes. Up to this time, he gave little or no evidence of contrition in his Diary.
He was now under deep domestic affliction. Of his thirteen children he had lost eight.
On the 25th of December, 1696, he buried his little Sarah, two years old, and on the 22d of
May previous an infant son. His Diary shows that his mind was in a state of abject
despondency. After the religious type of the period he regarded these repeated strokes
of Divine Providence as brought upon him by his own unworthiness. On the 11th of
January, three days before the appointed fast, he writes, "God helped me to pray more
"than ordinarily, that he would make up our loss in the burial of our little daughter and
"other children, and that [he] would give us a child to serve him, pleading with him as
"the institutor of marriage, and the author of every good work."

Calef (p. 144) gives an abstract from memory of Judge Sewall's confession; and Dr.
Abiel Holmes, who had seen the Diary, gives, in *American Annals* (vol. ii. p. 9), a brief extract. The following, copied, by permission, from his original Diary now in possession of
the Massachusetts Historical Society, is the paper entire:

N. B.
Bill
put up
at Fast.

"Copy of the Bill I put up on the Fast Day, giving it to Mr. Willard as he
"passed by, and standing up at the reading of it, and bowing when finished, in
"the afternoon.
"Samuel Sewall, sensible of the reiterated strokes of God upon himself and
"family; and being sensible, that as to the guilt contracted upon the opening of the
"late Commission of Oyer and Terminer, at Salem (to which the order of this day
"relates), he is, upon many accounts, more concerned than any that he knows of, desires

ton being informed of this act of one of his brethren, remarked upon it, that for himself, when he sat in judgment he had the fear of God before his eyes, and gave his opinion according to the best of his understanding, and although it might appear afterwards that he had been in an error, he saw no necessity of a public acknowledgment of it. One of the ministers,

" to take the blame and shame of it; asking pardon of men, and especially desiring prayers " that God, who has an unlimited authority, would pardon that sin, and all other his sins, " personal and relative: and according to his infinite benignity and sovereignty, not visit " the sin of him, or of any other, upon himself or any of his, nor upon the land: but that " he would powerfully defend him against all temptations to sin, for the future; and " vouchsafe him the efficacious, saving conduct of his word and spirit."
The following entry is the first indication I find in his diary, of sensitiveness or compunction for the part he took in the witchcraft trials.   It was made December 24, 1696, while his little Sarah lay dead in his house: " Sam [his son] recites to me, in Latin, Mat-" thew xii. from the 6th to the end of the 12th verse.   The 7th verse [Quod si nossetis quid " sit, misericordiam volo, et non sacrificium, non condemnassetis inculpabiles] did awfully " bring to mind the Salem tragedy."
The entire confession of Judge Sewall, its date and attending circumstances, will correct erroneous impressions concerning it.   The subject matter confessed covers but one point: " the guilt contracted upon the opening of the late commission of Oyer and Terminer at " Salem."   The court was opened June 2, 1692.   We cannot be in doubt as to the nature of the guilt then contracted.   It was the adoption of a rule of the court, by which the records made, and depositions received, at the preliminary examinations (which consisted almost wholly of spectral evidence), were introduced, sworn to, and received as legal testimony in the trials of the accused.   Out of this rule, which was wholly illegal, grew all the fatal results of the Salem trials.   Judge Sewall was a parishioner of Samuel Willard, of the Old South Church in Boston, who regarded such evidence as the " Devil's testimony "; and whose judicious conduct during the trials is worthy of the highest commendation.   He was the intimate friend of Increase and Cotton Mather, who both held similar views.   Three days before (March 31), Cotton Mather had written to John Richards, one of the judges, cautioning him against the use of spectral testimony.   The letter, although addressed to his own parishioner, was doubtless intended for, and considered by, the whole court, and is called, by himself and his son, the " letter to the judges."   The letter says: " If man-" kind have thus far once consented unto the credit of diabolical representations, the door " is opened for the devils to obtain, from the courts in the invisible world, a license to pro-" ceed unto most hideous desolations upon the repute and repose of such as have been kept " from the great transgression.   Perhaps there are wise and good men, that may be ready " to style him that shall advance this caution, a witch advocate ; but, in the winding up, " this caution will certainly be wished for."   (Mass. Soc.'s Hist. Coll., xxxviii. p, 393.)   In the face of such influences and associations Judge Sewall gave his voice in the court for legalizing spectral testimony !
But for his confession we might never have known the position of Judge Sewall on the matter of spectral evidence, then the great question of debate in the Province; or have surmised the position of his three Boston associates, Richards, Winthrop and Sergeant, Saltonstall, living in Haverhill, did not attend the sittings of the court.   The views of chief justice Stoughton in favor of admitting spectral testimony are well known ; and those of the three Salem members of the commission, Hathorne, Corwin and Gedney, we have before us in the records of their examinations, than which nothing more atrocious can be imagined. If the four Boston members had stood out against the views of Stoughton and the Salem members, there had been a tie in the commission.   Judge Sewall says, that, in the guilt contracted, " he is, upon many accounts, more concerned than any that he knows of." How can this be ?   Was it a morbid utterance of his desponding mind ; or has it an historical significance ?   He was not at the head of the court, nor its most influential member. Nothing appears to show that he was zealous, as Stoughton was, on this point.   The remark would be explained, if he alone, of the Boston judges, went over to Stoughton's views; and, by a majority vote, fixed the policy of the court.   I know of no evidence outside the confession to sustain this hypothesis; and it is here thrown out only for the purpose of eliciting further information as to the position of the other three Boston judges.   Brattle intimates that the members of the court were not a unit in their views.   He says, " But although

who in the time of it approved of the court's proceeding, remarked in his diary soon after that many were of opinion innocent blood had been shed. The afflicted were never brought to trial for their imposture. Many of them are said to have proved profligate, abandoned people, and others to have passed the remainder of their lives in a state of obscurity and contempt.[57]

" the chief judge and *some of the other judges* be very zealous in these proceedings," &c. I have seen no evidence that Richards, Winthrop, or Sergeant, after the policy of the court was fixed, did not sustain the action of their associates. The two theories respecting diabolical agency, which were then the subject of debate, I have treated at some length in *North American Review*, vol. cviii. pp. 337–397. P.

[57] October 17, 1711, the General Court passed an act reversing "the several convictions, "judgments, and attainders against the" persons executed, and several who were condemned but not executed, and declaring that to be null and void. In December of the same year, £578. 12s. were appropriated to pay the damages sustained by persons prosecuted for witchcraft in 1692. The act reversing the attainder shows that the popular belief in the diabolical nature of the witchcraft troubles had not abated twenty years after those events transpired. The act is in *Records of Salem Witchcraft*, vol. ii. pp. 216–218. It commences thus: "Forasmuch as in the year of our Lord 1692, two several towns within " this Province were infested with a horrible witchcraft, or possession of devils," &c. "The " influence and energy of the evil spirits so great at that time acting in and upon those who " were the principal accusers and witnesses;" and that "some of the principal accusers " and witnesses in those dark and severe prosecutions have since discovered themselves to " be persons of profligate and vicious conversation"—were the reasons assigned for the reversal of the attainder.

As showing Gov. Hutchinson's latest opinions on the question, whether the manifestations at Salem village were wholly the result of fraud and imposture, I append a supplementary paragraph with which he closes the narrative in his final draft.

" The opinion which prevailed in New-England for many years after this tragedy, that there " was something preternatural in it, and that it was not all the effect of fraud and imposture, " proceeded from the reluctance in human nature to reject errors once imbibed. As the " principal actors went off the stage this opinion was gradually lessened; but perhaps it " was owing to a respect to the memory of their immediate ancestor, that many do not " seem to be fully convinced. There are a great number of persons who are willing to sup- " pose the accusers to have been under bodily disorders which affected their imaginations. " This is kind and charitable, but seems to be winking the truth out of sight. A little at- " tention must force conviction that the whole was a scene of fraud and imposture begun " by young girls, who at first, perhaps, thought of nothing more than being pitied and in- " dulged, and continued by adult persons who were afraid of being accused themselves. " The one and the other, rather than confess their fraud, suffered the lives of so many in- " nocents to be taken away through the credulity of judges and juries." P.

ERRATUM.—The reference, in the text, to Note 49, should have been placed after the word "proceeded," at the end of the first sentence of the paragraph. P.

8

www.ingramcontent.com/pod-product-compliance
Lightning Source LLC
Chambersburg PA
CBHW021445090426
42739CB00009B/1651